CIMA
PRACTICE & REVISION KIT

Foundation Paper 3a
Economics for Business

BPP Professional Education
January 2004

First edition 2001
Fourth edition January 2004

ISBN 0 7517 1500 X (previous edition 0 7517 0275 7)

British Library Cataloguing-in-Publication Data
A catalogue record for this book
is available from the British Library

Published by

BPP Professional Education
Aldine House, Aldine Place
London W12 8AW

www.bpp.com

Printed in Great Britain by W M Print
45-47 Frederick Street
Walsall, West Midlands
WS2 9NE

All our rights reserved. No part of this publication may be reproduced, stored in a retrieval system or transmitted, in any form or by any means, electronic, mechanical, photocopying, recording or otherwise, without the prior written permission of BPP Professional Education.

We are grateful to the Chartered Institute of Management Accountants for permission to reproduce past examination questions. The answers to past examination questions have been prepared by BPP Professional Education.

©
BPP Professional Education
2004

CONTENTS

Revision

	Page number
Revising with this Kit	(iv)
Effective revision	(vi)

The assessment

Assessment technique	(ix)
Tackling multiple choice questions	(xi)
Tackling objective test questions	(xii)

Background

Useful websites	(xiv)
Syllabus mindmap	(xv)

Question and answer checklist/index (xvi)

	Questions	Answers
Question practice		
Multiple choice and objective test questions	3	79
Exam practice		
Mock assessment 1	113	123
Mock assessment 2	129	137

Order form

Review form & free prize draw

Revising with this Kit

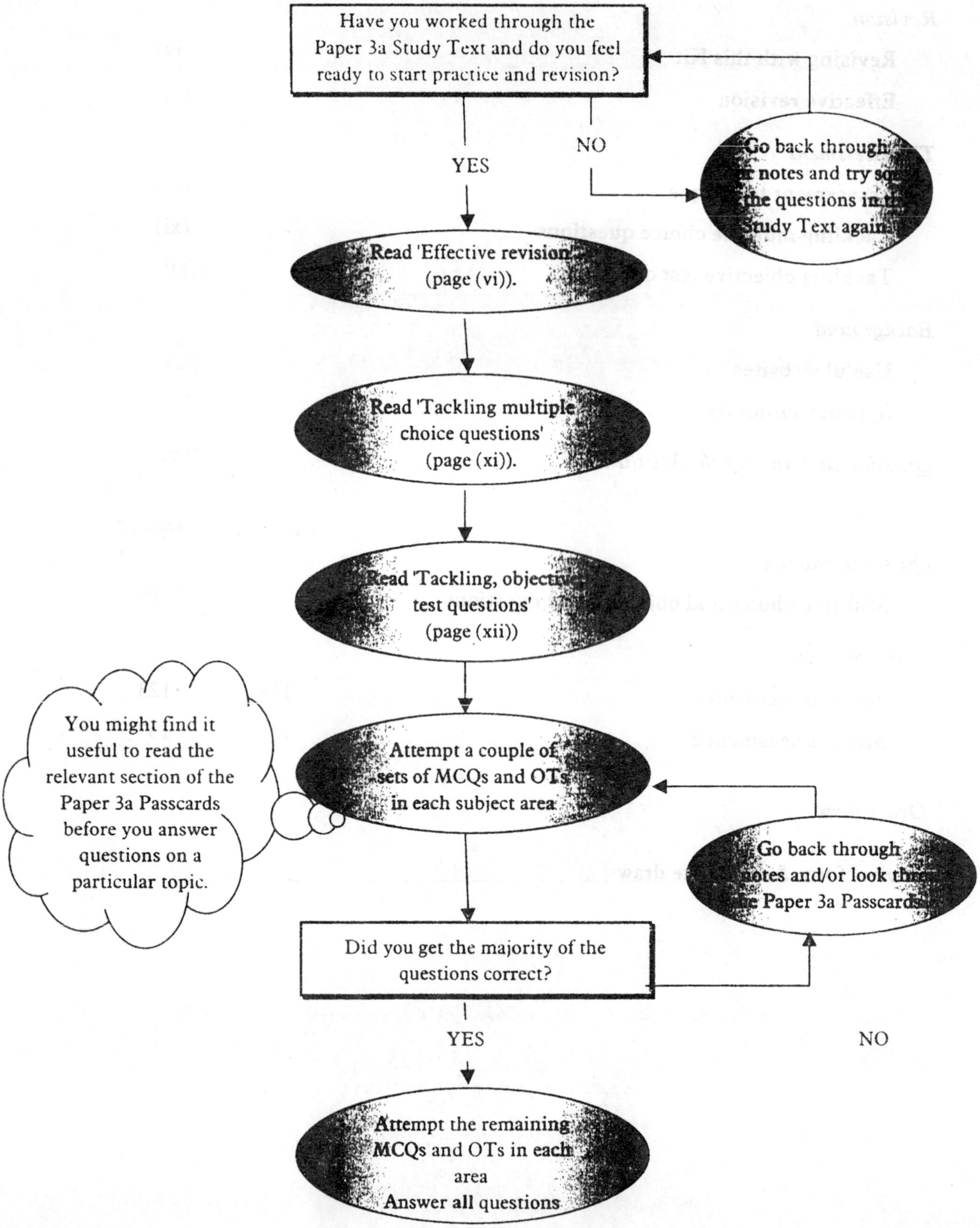

REVISING WITH THIS KIT

```
┌─────────────────────────────────┐
│ Have you worked through the     │
│ Paper 3a Study Text and do you  │
│ feel ready to start practice    │
│ and revision?                   │
└─────────────────────────────────┘
       │ YES          │ NO  →  ( Go back through
       ▼                        notes and try some
   ( Read 'Effective revision'    of the questions in the
     (page (vi)) )                Study Text again )
       │
       ▼
   ( Read 'Tackling multiple
     choice questions'
     (page (xi)) )
       │
       ▼
   ( Read 'Tackling objective
     test questions'
     (page (xii)) )
       │
       ▼
( You might find it useful to read the relevant section of the Paper 3a Passcards before you answer questions on a particular topic. )
   ──▶ ( Attempt a couple of sets of MCQs and OTs in each subject area )
       │
       ▼
┌─────────────────────────────────┐
│ Did you get the majority of the │
│ questions correct?              │
└─────────────────────────────────┘
       │ YES                │ NO  →  ( Go back through
       ▼                             notes and/or look through
   ( Attempt the remaining           the Paper 3a Passcards )
     MCQs and OTs in each
     area
     Answer all questions )
```

Revising with this Kit

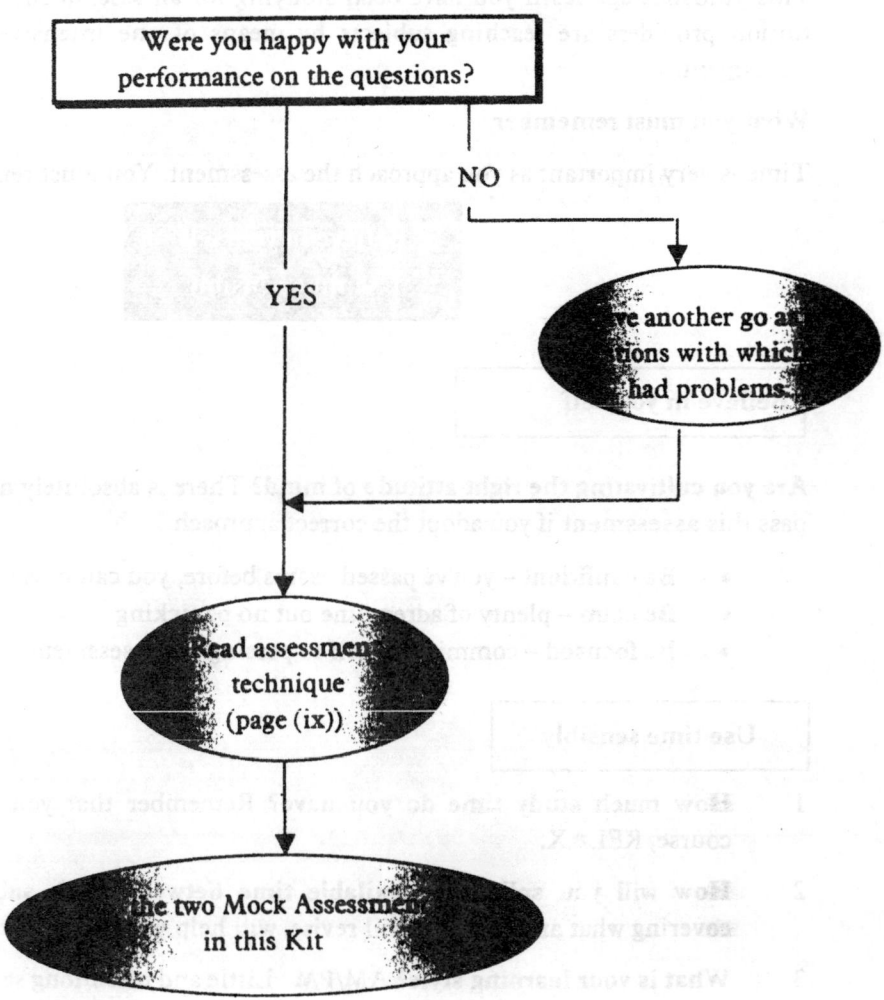

Effective revision

EFFECTIVE REVISION

This guidance applies if you have been studying for an assessment over a period of time. (Some tuition providers are teaching subjects by means of one intensive course that ends with the assessment.)

What you must remember

Time is very important as you approach the assessment. You must remember:

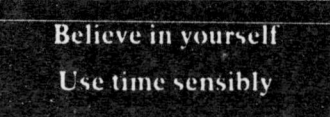

Believe in yourself

Are you cultivating the right attitude of mind? There is absolutely no reason why you should not pass this **assessment** if you adopt the correct approach.

- **Be confident** – you've passed exams before, you can pass them again
- **Be calm** – plenty of adrenaline but no panicking
- **Be focused** – commit yourself to passing the assessment

Use time sensibly

1. **How much study time do you have?** Remember that you must EAT, SLEEP, and of course, RELAX.

2. **How will you split that available time between each subject?** A revision timetable, covering what and how you will revise, will help you organise your revision thoroughly.

3. **What is your learning style?** AM/PM? Little and often/long sessions? Evenings/ weekends?

4. **Do you have quality study time?** Unplug the phone. Let everybody know that you're studying and shouldn't be disturbed.

5. **Are you taking regular breaks?** Most people absorb more if they do not attempt to study for long uninterrupted periods of time. A five minute break every hour (to make coffee, watch the news headlines) can make all the difference.

6. **Are you rewarding yourself for your hard work?** Are you leading a **healthy lifestyle**?

What to revise

Key topics

You need to spend **most time** on, and practise **lots of questions** on, topics that are likely to yield plenty of questions in your assessment.

You may also find certain areas of the syllabus difficult.

Difficult áreas are:
- Areas you find dull or pointless
- Subjects you highlighted as difficult when you studied them
- Topics that gave you problems when you answered questions or reviewed the material

DON'T become depressed about these areas; instead do something about them.

- Build up your knowledge by **quick tests** such as the quick quizzes in your BPP Study Text and the MCQ cards.
- Work carefully through **numerical examples** and **questions** in the Study Text, and refer back to the Text if you struggle with questions in this Kit.

Breadth of revision

Make sure your revision covers all areas of the syllabus. Your assessment will test your knowledge of the whole syllabus.

How to revise

There are four main ways that you can revise a topic area.

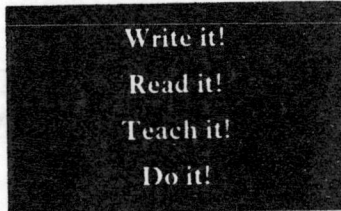

Write it!
Read it!
Teach it!
Do it!

Write it!

Writing important points down will help you recall them, particularly if your notes are presented in a way that makes it easy for you to remember them.

Read it!

You should read your notes or BPP Passcards actively, testing yourself by doing quick quizzes or Kit questions while you are reading.

Teach it!

Assessments require you to show your understanding. Teaching what you are learning to another person helps you practise explaining topics that you might be asked to define in your assessment. Teaching someone who will challenge your understanding, someone for example who will be taking the same assessment as you, can be helpful to both of you.

Effective revision

> Do it!

Remember that you are revising in order to be able to answer questions in the assessment. Practising questions will help you practise **technique** and **discipline**, which can be crucial in passing or failing assessments.

1. Start your question practice by doing a couple of sets of multiple choice questions and objective test questions in a subject area. Note down the questions where you went wrong, try to identify why you made mistakes and go back to your Study Text for guidance or practice.

2. The **more questions** you do, the more likely you are to pass the assessment. However if you do run short of time:
    - Make sure that you have done at least some questions from every section of the syllabus
    - Look through the banks of multiple choice questions and objective test questions and do questions on areas that you have found difficult or on which you have made mistakes

3. When you think you can successfully answer questions on the whole syllabus, attempt the **two Mock Assessments** at the end of this Kit. You will get the most benefit by sitting them under strict assessment conditions, so that you gain experience of the vital assessment processes.
    - Managing your time
    - Producing answers

BPP's *Learning to Learn Accountancy* gives further valuable advice on how to approach revision.

BPP has also produced other useful revision aids.

- **Passcards** – Provide you with clear topic summaries and assessment tips
- **MCQ Cards** – Prepare you for answering multiple choice questions by giving you lots and lots of practice
- **i-Pass CDs** – Offer you tests of knowledge to be completed against the clock
- **Success CDs and Success Tapes** – Help you revise on the move

You can purchase these products by completing the order form at the back of this Kit or by visiting www.bpp.com/cima

ASSESSMENT TECHNIQUE

Format of the assessment

The assessment will contain 40 objective test questions to be completed in one hour. The questions may be a combination of multiple choice questions and other types of objective test questions. The mark allocation may vary between different questions.

Passing assessments

Passing assessments is half about having the knowledge, and half about doing yourself full justice in the assessment. You must have the right approach to two things.

> **The day of the assessment**
> **Your time in the assessment room**

The day of the assessment

1. Set at least one **alarm** (or get an alarm call) for a morning assessment.
2. Have **something to eat** but beware of eating too much; you may feel sleepy if your system is digesting a large meal.
3. Allow plenty of **time to get to the assessment room**; have your route worked out in advance and listen to news bulletins to check for potential travel problems.
4. **Don't forget** pens and watch. Also make sure you remember **entrance documentation** and **evidence of identity**.
5. Put **new batteries** into your calculator and take a spare set (or a spare calculator).
6. **Avoid discussion** about the assessment with other candidates outside the assessment room.

Your time in the assessment room

1. *Listen carefully to the invigilator's instructions*

   Make sure you understand the formalities you have to complete.

2. *Ensure you follow the instructions on the computer screen*

   In particular ensure that you select the correct assessment (not every student does!), and that you understand how to work through the assessment and submit your answers.

3. *Keep your eye on the time*

   In the assessment you will have to complete 40 questions in 60 minutes. That will mean that you have roughly one and a half minutes on average to answer each question. However you will be able to answer some questions instantly, but others will require working out. If after a couple of minutes you have no idea how to tackle the question, leave it and come back to it later.

4. *Label your workings clearly with the question number*

   This will help you when you check your answers, or if you come back to a question that you are unsure about.

Assessment technique

5   *Deal with problem questions*

There are two ways of dealing with questions where you are unsure of the answer.

(a) **Don't submit an answer.** The computer will tell you before you move to the next question that you have not submitted an answer, and the question will be marked as not done on the list of questions. The risk with this approach is that you run out of time before you do submit an answer.

(b) **Submit an answer.** You can always come back and change the answer before you finish the assessment or the time runs out. You should though make a note of answers that you are unsure about, to ensure that you do revisit them later in the assessment.

6   *Make sure you submit an answer for every question*

When there are ten minutes left to go, concentrate on submitting answers for all the questions that you have not answered up to that point. You won't get penalised for wrong answers so take a guess if you're unsure.

7   *Check your answers*

If you finish the assessment with time to spare, check your answers before you sign out of the assessment. In particular revisit questions that you are unsure about, and check that your answers are in the right format and contain the correct number of words as appropriate.

BPP's *Learning to Learn Accountancy* gives further valuable advice on how to approach the day of the assessment.

TACKLING MULTIPLE CHOICE QUESTIONS

The MCQs in your assessment contain a number of possible answers. You have to **choose the option(s) that best answers the question**. The three incorrect options are called distracters. There is a skill in answering MCQs quickly and correctly. By practising MCQs you can develop this skill, giving you a better chance of passing the assessment.

You may wish to follow the approach outlined below, or you may prefer to adapt it.

Step 1. **Note down how long you should allocate to each MCQ.** For this paper you will be answering 40 questions in 60 minutes, so you will be spending on average one and a half minutes on each question. Remember however that you will not be expected to spend an equal amount of time on each MCQ; some can be answered instantly but others will take time to work out.

Step 2. **Attempt each question. Read the question thoroughly.**

You may find that you recognise a question when you sit the assessment. Be aware that the detail and/or requirement may be different. If the question seems familiar read the requirement and options carefully – do not assume that it is identical.

Step 3. Read the four options and see if one matches your own answer. Be careful with numerical questions, as the distracters are designed to match answers that incorporate **common errors**. Check that your calculation is correct. Have you followed the requirement exactly? Have you included every stage of the calculation?

Step 4. You may find that none of the options matches your answer.

- **Re-read the question** to ensure that you understand it and are answering the requirement
- **Eliminate any obviously wrong answers**
- **Consider which of the remaining answers** is the most likely to be correct and select the option

Step 5. If you are still unsure, **continue to the next question**. Likewise if you are nowhere near working out which option is correct after a couple of minutes, leave the question and come back to it later. Make a note of any questions for which you have submitted answers, but you need to return to later. The computer will list any questions for which you have not submitted answers.

Step 6. **Revisit questions** you are uncertain about. When you come back to a question after a break you often find you are able to answer it correctly straight away. If you are still unsure have a guess. You are not penalised for incorrect answers, so **never leave a question unanswered!**

TACKLING OBJECTIVE TEST QUESTIONS

What is an objective test question?

An objective test (**OT**) question is made up of some form of **stimulus**, usually a question, and a **requirement** to do something.

- **MCQs.** Read through the information on page (xi) about MCQs and how to tackle them.
- **Data entry.** This type of OT requires you to provide figures such as the correct figure for creditors in a balance sheet.
- **Hot spots.** This question format might ask you to identify which cell on a spreadsheet contains a particular formula or where on a graph marginal revenue equals marginal cost.
- **Multiple response.** These questions provide you with a number of options and you have to identify those that fulfil certain criteria.
- **Matching.** This OT question format could ask you to classify particular costs into one of a range of cost classifications provided, to match descriptions of variances with one of a number of variances listed, and so on.

OT questions in your assessment

CIMA is currently developing different types of OTs for inclusion in computer-based assessments. It is not certain how many questions in your assessment will be MCQs, and how many will be other types of OT. Practising all the different types of OTs that this Kit provides will prepare you well for whatever questions come up in your assessment.

Dealing with OT questions

Again you may wish to follow the approach we suggest, or you may be prepared to adopt it.

Step 1. Work out **how long** you should allocate to each OT. Remember that you will not be expected to spend an equal amount of time on each one; some can be answered instantly but others will take time to work out.

Step 2. **Attempt each question.** Read the question thoroughly, and note in particular what the question says about the **format** of your answer and whether there are any **restrictions** placed on it (for example the number of words you can use).

You may find that you recognise a question when you sit the assessment. Be aware that the detail and/or requirement may be different. If the question seems familiar read the requirement and options carefully – do not assume that it is identical.

Step 3. Read any options you are given and select which ones are appropriate. Check that your calculations are correct. Have you followed the requirement exactly? Have you included every stage of the calculation?

Step 4. You may find that you are unsure of the answer.

- Re-read the question to ensure that you understand it and are answering the requirement

(xii)

Tackling objective test questions

- Eliminate any obviously wrong options if you are given a number of options from which to choose
- Consider which of any remaining answers is the most likely to be correct and select the option

Step 5. If you are still unsure, **continue to the next question**. Likewise if you are nowhere near working out which option is correct after a couple of minutes, leave the question and come back to it later. Make a note of any questions for which you have submitted answers, but you need to return to later. The computer will list any questions for which you have not submitted answers.

Step 6. Revisit questions you are uncertain about. When you come back to a question after a break you often find you are able to answer it correctly straight away. If you are still unsure have a guess. You are not penalised for incorrect answers, so **never leave a question unanswered!**

USEFUL WEBSITES

The websites below provide additional sources of information of relevance to your studies for *Economics for Business*.

- BPP www.bpp.com

  For details of other BPP material for your CIMA studies

- CIMA www.cimaglobal.com

  The official CIMA website

- *Financial Times* www.ft.com

  Essential background reading, as recommended by the examiner

- *The Economist* www.economist.com

  Background material as recommended by the examiner

- *Wall Street Journal* www.wsj.com

  For a different financial perspective

- www.tutor2u.net

  Briefings, study notes and data for A level economics

- www.bized.ac.uk

  Business and economics learning resources

- http://netec.mcc.ac.uk/JokEc.html

  Economics background material

SYLLABUS MINDMAP

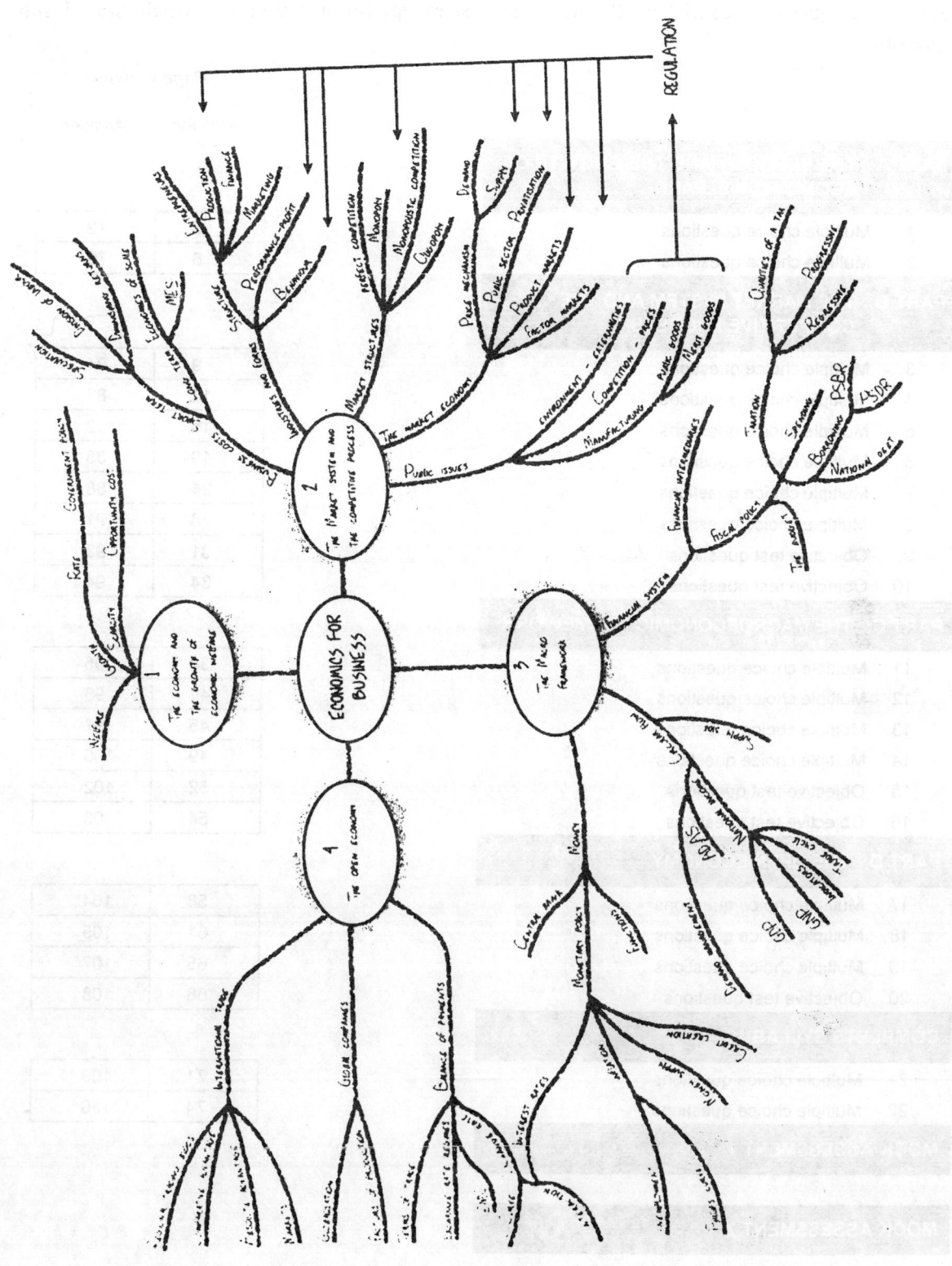

QUESTION AND ANSWER CHECKLIST/INDEX

The headings in this checklist/index indicate the main topics of questions.

All sets of questions consist of 20 sub-questions, except for question 15, which has 15 sub-questions.

Page number

			Question	Answer

PART A: THE ECONOMY AND THE GROWTH OF ECONOMIC WELFARE

		Question	Answer
1	Multiple choice questions	3	79
2	Multiple choice questions	6	79

PART B: THE MARKET SYSTEM AND THE COMPETITIVE PROCESS

		Question	Answer
3	Multiple choice questions	9	81
4	Multiple choice questions	12	82
5	Multiple choice questions	15	82
6	Multiple choice questions	19	85
7	Multiple choice questions	24	88
8	Multiple choice questions	28	91
9	Objective test questions	31	93
10	Objective test questions	34	94

PART C: THE MACROECONOMIC FRAMEWORK

		Question	Answer
11	Multiple choice questions	38	95
12	Multiple choice questions	41	96
13	Multiple choice questions	45	97
14	Multiple choice questions	49	100
15	Objective test questions	52	102
16	Objective test questions	54	103

PART D: THE OPEN ECONOMY

		Question	Answer
17	Multiple choice questions	58	104
18	Multiple choice questions	61	105
19	Multiple choice questions	65	107
20	Objective test questions	68	108

COMPLETE SYLLABUS

		Question	Answer
21	Multiple choice questions	71	109
22	Multiple choice questions	74	110

MOCK ASSESSMENT 1

MOCK ASSESSMENT 2

Questions

Questions: The economy and the growth of economic welfare

THE ECONOMY AND THE GROWTH OF ECONOMIC WELFARE

The sets of questions 1 and 2 cover the economy and the growth of economic welfare, the subject of Part A of the BPP Study Text for Paper 3a.

1 MULTIPLE CHOICE QUESTIONS

1 The opportunity cost of constructing a road is:

   A   The money spent on the construction of the road

   B   The value of goods and services that could otherwise have been produced with the resources used to build the road

   C   The cost of the traffic congestion caused during the construction of the road

   D   The value of goods that could have been produced with the labour employed in the construction of the road

2 In a market economy, the allocation of resources between different productive activities is determined mainly by the:

   A   Decisions of the government
   B   Wealth of entrepreneurs
   C   Pattern of consumer expenditure
   D   Supply of factors of production

3 Which one of the following best describes the opportunity cost to society of building a new school?

   A   The increased taxation to pay for the school

   B   The money that was spent on building the school

   C   The other goods that could have been produced with the resources used to build the school

   D   The running cost of the school when it is opened

4 In a market economy the price system provides all of the following except which *one*?

   A   An estimation of the value placed on goods by consumers
   B   A distribution of income according to needs
   C   Incentives to producers
   D   A means of allocating resources between different uses

5 The 'central economic problem' means:

   A   The output of goods and services is limited by scarce resources
   B   Market prices do not always equal costs of production
   C   All businesses must make a profit
   D   Consumers cannot maximise their utility because of limited information

6 The term 'mixed economy' implies all of the following conditions except which *one*?

   A   The allocation of resources is mainly through the price system.
   B   Producers have an incentive to advertise their products.
   C   There is some government planning of the use of resources.
   D   All industries have a mix of small and large companies.

3

Questions: The economy and the growth of economic welfare

7   Which one of the following statements is *not* true?

    A   The basic economic problem is the same in planned and free market economies.
    B   The basic economic problem is one of choice between alternatives.
    C   Factors of production are limited in supply.
    D   Choice is necessary because of limited consumer wants.

8   When a government wishes to increase its expenditure on education but can do so only at the expense of expenditure elsewhere, this is an example of:

    A   Diminishing marginal utility
    B   Opportunity cost
    C   Scale of preferences
    D   Equi-marginal returns

9   Which of the following does *not* help to determine the rate of growth of a country's potential output?

    A   The economic resources available to it
    B   Its rate of technological change
    C   The opportunity cost of its products
    D   The level of business confidence

10   Which of the following is *not* a likely consequence of economic growth?

    A   More rapid depletion of material resources
    B   Structural unemployment
    C   Increased levels of externalities
    D   Reduced provision of public goods

11   Which one of the following is *not* a characteristic of a mixed economy?

    A   Weights and measures legislation
    B   Employment protection legislation
    C   Oligopolies in some industries
    D   Absence of a stock market

12   The basic economic problem facing all economies is:

    A   Economic growth
    B   Unemployment
    C   Inflation
    D   Scarcity of resources

13   In a planned economy, the pattern of production is determined by:

    A   Central allocation
    B   Consumer preference
    C   The price mechanism
    D   The profit motive

14   In a free market economy, the price mechanism:

    A   Aids government control
    B   Allocates resources
    C   Reduces unfair competition
    D   Measures national wealth

Questions: The economy and the growth of economic welfare

15 Which of the following would be regarded as a part of the secondary sector of industry?

   A   Farming
   B   Quarrying
   C   Engineering
   D   Banking

16 Which of the following is *not* an indicator of growing national income?

   A   An increase in exports
   B   A rise in unemployment benefit payments
   C   A rise in consumption
   D   Shortages of some types of labour

17 Opportunity cost is:

   A   The cost of producing one extra unit of the commodity
   B   The lowest average cost of the commodity
   C   The total cost of the commodity
   D   The loss of the next best alternative

18 Which of the following best describes the opportunity cost of a programme of immunisation?

   A   The actuarial valuation of the lives of those who are protected against the disease
   B   The cost of the vaccine
   C   The cost of providing the medical staff
   D   The work the medical staff cannot undertake as a result of the programme

19 In the production possibility diagram below, what would be the probable effect on living standards of moving from point A to point B?

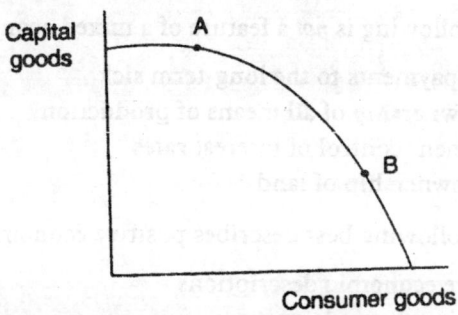

   A   Reduced now, improved in future
   B   Reduced now, reduced in future
   C   Improved now, reduced in future
   D   Improved now, improved in future

20 Which *one* of the following would *not* shift a country's production possibility frontier outwards (further away from the origin)?

   A   An increase in exports
   B   Technical progress reducing production costs
   C   An increase in the working population
   D   An improvement in the literacy rate

Notes Questions: The economy and the growth of economic welfare

2 MULTIPLE CHOICE QUESTIONS

1 Which *one* of the following government policies would *not* tend to raise the long-term rate of economic growth upwards?

    A   Increasing the qualifying age for state pension
    B   Providing tax incentives for the purchase of machinery by businesses
    C   Extending the motorway network
    D   Reducing the tax rate on restaurant meals

2 Which *one* of the following is *not* a social cost?

    A   Alcohol-related violence
    B   Compensation paid by a company to a customer
    C   Stress caused by unemployment
    D   Stress caused by overwork

3 Which of the following is *most likely* to lead directly to a productivity increase in a firm?

    A   Employing more labour
    B   Investing in product research
    C   Employing less labour
    D   Streamlining production processes

4 Which *one* of the following is *not* associated with conditions of economic growth?

    A   An increase in the volume of consumption
    B   An increase in the rate of saving
    C   An increase in value added
    D   An increase in real earnings

5 Which of the following is *not* a feature of a mixed economy?

    A   Welfare payments to the long-term sick
    B   Public ownership of all means of production
    C   Government control of interest rates
    D   Private ownership of land

6 Which of the following best describes positive economics?

    A   Objective economic descriptions
    B   Economic value judgements
    C   Description of economic units
    D   Description of economic aggregates

7 Which of the following would *not* be regarded by economists as a factor of production?

    A   Labour
    B   Enterprise
    C   Management
    D   Capital

8 Which of the following branches of economic study is concerned with value judgements and opinion as to what ought to happen in an ideal economy?

    A   Positive economics
    B   Normative economics
    C   Both positive economics and normative economics
    D   Neither positive economics nor normative economics

Questions: The economy and the growth of economic welfare

9 Which of the following would be *unlikely* to lead to an outward movement of a nation's production possibility frontier (curve)?

    A   An increase in productivity per worker
    B   The repeal of maximum working hours laws
    C   Net emigration
    D   A rising birth rate

10 The participation rate is:

    A   The rate of growth of the workforce
    B   The economic growth rate unadjusted for inflation
    C   The potential growth rate of the economy
    D   The proportion of the population that contributes to measured output

11 Which of the following features of economic activity can be used as evidence in arguments against promoting economic growth?

    A   Externalities
    B   Extraction of natural resources
    C   Requirement for new skills
    D   All of the above (A, B and C)

12 Consider the production possibility curve for the country of Fantasia, shown below. The Fantasian economy is currently operating at point D.

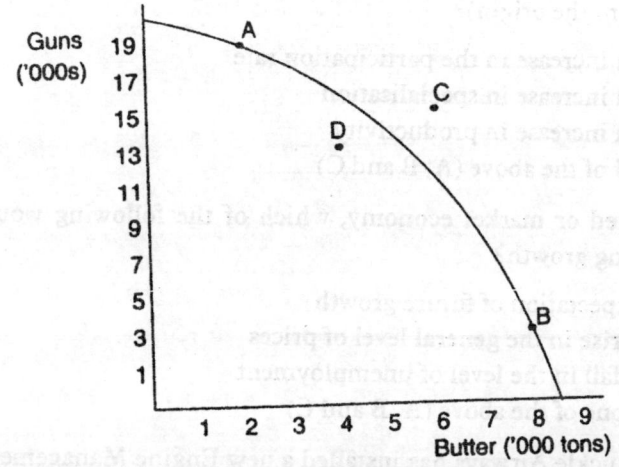

If Fantasia gave up the production of 4,000 guns, how many extra thousand tons of butter could it expect to produce, assuming it used all its resources efficiently?

    A   About 2.7
    B   About 6.7
    C   About 1.5
    D   Zero

13 Which of the following will move an economy's production possibility curve (frontier) outwards (away from the origin)?

    A   A reduction in unemployment
    B   A fall in prices
    C   A rise in prices
    D   None of the above

Notes   Questions: The economy and the growth of economic welfare

14 In a centrally planned economy:

   A   Choices about resource allocation are made by the government
   B   There is no role for money
   C   GNP is likely to be much higher than in a market economy of similar resource endowment
   D   All of the above (A, B and C)

15 An economic system in which both market forces and government planning play a part and in which there is both individual wealth and a government-provided welfare system is called:

   A   A democracy
   B   A mixed economy
   C   A market economy
   D   A common market

16 Economic value (exchange value) depends upon:

   A   The size of the money supply
   B   Specialisation
   C   Scarcity
   D   None of the above

17 Which of the following is likely to shift the production possibility frontier outwards (away from the origin)?

   A   An increase in the participation rate
   B   An increase in specialisation
   C   An increase in productivity
   D   All of the above (A, B and C)

18 In a mixed or market economy, which of the following would tend to contribute to continuing growth?

   A   Expectation of future growth
   B   A rise in the general level of prices
   C   A fall in the level of unemployment
   D   None of the above (A, B and C)

19 Whiteknuckle Airways has installed a new Engine Management System in its airliners, enabling the airline to reduce the number of cockpit crew from three to two on flights of less than eight hours' duration. This is an example of:

   A   Increased specialisation
   B   A fall in the participation rate
   C   Increased labour productivity
   D   All of the above (A, B and C)

20 Economic growth tends to be higher in the USA than in the EU mainly because:

   A   The USA has a smaller population than the EU
   B   The USA is more technically advanced than the EU
   C   The USA has a greater control over its labour force than the EU
   D   None of the above (A, B and C)

THE MARKET SYSTEM AND THE COMPETITIVE PROCESS

The sets of questions 3 to 10 cover the market system and the competitive process, the subject of Part B of the BPP Study Text for Paper 3a.

3 MULTIPLE CHOICE QUESTIONS

1 Which one of the following would cause the supply curve for a good to shift to the right (outwards from the origin)?

   A   A fall in the price of the good
   B   An increase in the demand for the good
   C   A fall in production costs of the good
   D   The imposition of a minimum price

2 When the price of a good is held above the equilibrium price, the result will be

   A   Excess demand
   B   A shortage of the good
   C   A surplus of the good
   D   An increase in demand

3 If the price of a good fell by 10% and, as a result, total expenditure on the good fell by 10%, the demand for the good would be described as:

   A   Perfectly inelastic
   B   Perfectly elastic
   C   Unitary elastic
   D   Elastic

4 Which one of the following would not lead directly to a shift in the demand curve for overseas holidays?

   A   An advertising campaign by holiday tour operators
   B   A fall in the disposable incomes of consumers
   C   A rise in the price of domestic holidays
   D   A rise in the exchange rate for the domestic country's currency

5 There is a rise in wage rates in an industry. Which one of the following will limit the amount of unemployment caused by the wage rise?

   A   The supply of substitute factors of production is inelastic
   B   Labour costs form a high proportion of total costs
   C   The demand for the industry's product is very price elastic
   D   Labour and capital are easily substituted for each other

6 Which of the following best describes the law of diminishing returns?

   As more labour is added to a fixed amount of capital:

   A   Total output will fall
   B   Increases in total output will become smaller for each additional unit of labour employed
   C   The marginal revenue from each additional unit of output produced will decline
   D   Production costs will rise because higher wages will have to be paid to attract more labour

Questions: The market system and the competitive process

7 Which one of the following is not a source of economies of scale?

   A   The introduction of specialist capital equipment
   B   Bulk buying
   C   The employment of specialist managers
   D   Cost savings resulting from new production techniques

8 Which of the following are characteristics of perfect competition?

   (i)   Large numbers of producers
   (ii)   Differentiated goods
   (iii) The absence of long-run excess profits
   (iv)   Freedom of entry to and exit from the industry

   A   (i), (ii) and (iii) only
   B   (i), (iii) and (iv) only
   C   (ii), (iii) and (iv) only
   D   All of them

9 Which one of the following is not a feature of an industry operating under conditions of monopolistic competition?

   A   There is product differentiation.
   B   Producers operate at below full capacity output.
   C   Firms maximise profits where marginal cost equals marginal revenue.
   D   There is one dominant producer.

10 Which of the following is likely to lead to a fall in the price of good Q?

   A   A rise in the price of good P, a substitute for good Q
   B   A fall in the level of household incomes generally
   C   A fall in the price of good T, a complement to good Q
   D   A belief that the price of good Q is likely to double in the next 3 months

11 All of the following are characteristics of a market displaying perfect competition *except* which *one*?

   A   The product is homogeneous but differentiated by advertising.
   B   There are no information gathering costs.
   C   Producers act rationally.
   D   There is a large number of sellers in the market.

12 The demand curve for a product will shift to the left when there is:

   A   A rise in household income
   B   An increase in the product's desirability from the point of view of fashion
   C   A fall in the price of a substitute
   D   A fall in the price of a complement

13 Which of the following is *not* a factor reward?

   A   An in-work welfare payment
   B   The discount on a bill of exchange
   C   The increased value of a share option
   D   A repayment by the government of tax overpaid

14 Which of the following goods is not complementary to the service of picture framing?

   A   Rented accommodation
   B   Timber suitable for making picture frames
   C   Picture hooks
   D   Photographic film

10

Questions: The market system and the competitive process

15 Which of the following is not a substitute for carpet?

    A   Ceramic floor tiles
    B   Varnish
    C   Vinyl flooring
    D   Underfloor heating

16 Which of the following is not a complement to carpets?

    A   A vacuum cleaner
    B   Carpet fitting service
    C   Central heating
    D   Underlay

17 The demand for fashion goods is not influenced by:

    A   Price
    B   Allocative inefficiency among producers
    C   The distribution of income among households
    D   Expectation of future price changes

18 Oligopoly markets typically do not display price competition because:

    A   Barriers to entry exist
    B   Products are clearly differentiated
    C   Producers' decisions are interdependent
    D   There is always a price leader

19 A natural monopoly is characterised by:

    A   Being a major part of the primary sector
    B   Allocative inefficiency
    C   Allocative efficiency
    D   Very high average fixed costs

20 An individual firm in long term equilibrium in a perfect competitive market will produce at a level where:

    A   Marginal cost exceeds average cost
    B   Marginal cost is less than average cost
    C   Marginal cost and average cost are equal
    D   Marginal revenue is greater than average revenue

Questions: The market system and the competitive process

4 MULTIPLE CHOICE QUESTIONS

1. Which of the following most clearly constitutes a barrier to entry to an industry?

    A   The need for capital investment
    B   A high level of fixed costs
    C   The existence of diseconomies of scale
    D   The need to employ highly skilled labour

2. Which of the following arguments could *not* be used to support the existence of monopolies?

    A   Monopolies can achieve maximum economies of scale.
    B   Monopolists can practise price discrimination.
    C   Monopolies can finance more new projects out of profits.
    D   Monopoly is efficient in its use of resources.

3. A monopolist's average revenue curve always slopes downwards because:

    A   Economies of scale exist in distribution
    B   There are allocative inefficiencies
    C   Market demand increases as price falls
    D   Marginal revenue can be negative

4. A reduction in government regulation of industry is *unlikely* to produce which of the following undesirable effects?

    A   An increase in market imperfections
    B   Lower quality of service
    C   Cyclical unemployment
    D   Reduced provision of public goods

5. Regulatory capture occurs when:

    A   An indirect tax is imposed on imports
    B   Government imposes rationing during a crisis
    C   A regulator closes a loop hole
    D   Regulations favour producers rather than consumers

6. Which of the following is not a public good?

    A   An aircraft navigation radio beacon
    B   Pollination of crops by a bee-keeper's bees
    C   A public library
    D   Street lighting

7. If the demand for a good is *price elastic*, which one of the following is true?

    When the price of the good:

    A   Rises, the quantity demanded falls and total expenditure on the good increases
    B   Rises, the quantity demanded falls and total expenditure on the good decreases
    C   Falls, the quantity demanded rises and total expenditure on the good decreases
    D   Falls, the quantity demanded rises and total expenditure on the good is unchanged

8   Which of the following always rise when a manufacturing business increases its output?

    (i)   Fixed costs
    (ii)   Marginal cost
    (iii) Average variable cost
    (iv)   Total costs

    A   (i) and (ii) only
    B   (ii) and (iii) only
    C   (iii) and (iv) only
    D   (iv) only

9   The long-run average cost curve for a business will eventually rise because of:

    A   The law of diminishing returns
    B   Increasing competition in the industry
    C   Limits to the size of the market for the good
    D   Diseconomies of scale

10 The benefits to a company when it locates close to other companies in the same industry include all of the following *except* which one?

    A   The benefits of bulk buying
    B   The provision of specialist commercial services
    C   The development of dedicated transport and marketing facilities
    D   The supply of labour with relevant skills

11 Which one of the following statements about profit is correct?

    A   In the private sector, the profit motive encourages efficiency.
    B   Nationalised industries are always inefficient because they are not profit-motivated.
    C   Not-for-profit organisations do not have to worry about being efficient.
    D   In the private sector, companies cannot be profitable unless they are efficient.

12 In a perfectly competitive market, all producers charge the same price because:

    A   They are all profit maximisers
    B   They have the same costs
    C   The product is homogeneous
    D   All firms are small

13 Which of the following is *not* a merit good?

    A   A lighthouse
    B   Nursery education
    C   Immunisation against an epidemic disease
    D   Subsidised housing

14 Economic rent is:

    A   A transfer payment
    B   A payment to the lessor of an asset
    C   A payment in excess of the amount needed to keep a factor of production in its current use
    D   The price of land

Questions: The market system and the competitive process

15 Elasticity of demand for labour is influenced by *all* of the factors below except which *one*?

    A   The elasticity of supply of alternative factors of production
    B   The elasticity of supply of the final product
    C   The proportion of labour costs to total costs
    D   The ease of substituting other factors of production

16 The marginal efficiency of capital depends on:

    A   Prevailing interest rates
    B   The degree of automation
    C   The size of the most recent dividend
    D   The ease with which capital can be substituted for labour

17 The substitution effect of a wage rate increase affects the labour supply by:

    A   Attracting more productive labour
    B   Causing workers to substitute leisure for work
    C   Causing workers to substitute work for leisure
    D   Reducing the marginal physical product of labour

18 Immobility of labour may be caused by *all* of the following factors except which *one*?

    A   Accountancy exams
    B   Poor public transport
    C   Discrimination
    D   Cultural differences

19 Which *one* of the following would normally cause a rightward shift in the demand curve for a product?

    A   A fall in the price of a substitute product
    B   A reduction in direct taxation on incomes
    C   A reduction in price of the product
    D   An increase in the price of a complementary produce

20 If the price of coffee falls, which *one* of the following outcomes would be expected to occur?

    A   A fall in the quantity of coffee demanded
    B   A rise in the price of tea
    C   A fall in the demand for drinking cups
    D   A fall in the demand for tea

Questions: The market system and the competitive process

5 MULTIPLE CHOICE QUESTIONS

1 What is an inferior good?

   A   A good of such poor quality that demand for it is very weak

   B   A good of lesser quality than a substitute good, so that the price of the substitute is higher

   C   A good for which the cross elasticity of demand with a substitute product is greater than 1

   D   A good for which demand will fall as household income rises

2 Consider the price and demand for flower vases. The price of cut flowers goes up sharply. Which of the following would you expect to happen?

   A   The demand curve for flower vases will shift to the left and their price will rise

   B   The demand curve for flower vases will shift to the right and their price will rise

   C   There will be a movement along the demand curve for flower vases and their price will go down

   D   The demand curve for flower vases will shift to the left and their price will go down

3 Which of the following statements is true?

   Statement

   1   If the price elasticity of demand is more than 1, a fall in price will result in a fall in total expenditure on the product.

   2   The income elasticity of demand will only be zero in the case of inferior goods.

   3   The cross-elasticity of demand for complementary goods will always be positive.

   A   None of them is true.
   B   Statement 1 only is true.
   C   Statement 2 only is true.
   D   Statement 3 only is true.

4 The demand for a product will tend to be inelastic when:

   A   It has very few close substitutes
   B   It is very quickly consumed
   C   It tends to be purchased by people on subsistence incomes
   D   It has a wide range of different uses

5 The cross elasticity of demand between widgets and splodgets is 0.6 and the two goods are complements. The price of splodgets goes up by 10%, and demand for splodgets goes down by 15%. Which of the following will happen, in the short run time period?

   A   The equilibrium output and price of widgets will *both* fall, but we do not know what either of them will now be.

   B   The demand for widgets will go down by 6%, and the price of widgets will remain unchanged.

   C   The demand for widgets will go down by 9%, and the price of widgets will remain unchanged.

   D   The equilibrium output and price of widgets will change, with price above and quantity demanded below where they were before.

15

Questions: The market system and the competitive process

6 The demand for a product will tend to be elastic when:

   A   The product has a number of different uses
   B   The product is bought mainly by people on subsistence incomes
   C   The product has very few close substitutes
   D   The product is a non-durable consumer good that is quickly consumed

7 When a firm produces one extra unit of output, what is the marginal cost of the unit?

   1   The increase in total cost of production
   2   The increase in the variable cost of production
   3   The increase in the average cost of production

   A   Definition 1 only
   B   Definition 2 only
   C   Definition 3 only
   D   Definitions 1 and 2 only

8 Which of the following propositions are false?

   1   It is possible for the average total cost curve to be falling while the average variable cost curve is rising.
   2   It is possible for the average total cost curve to be rising while the average variable cost curve is falling.
   3   Marginal fixed costs per unit will fall as output increases.
   4   Marginal costs will be equal to marginal variable costs.

   A   Propositions 1 and 3 are false.
   B   Propositions 1 and 4 are false.
   C   Propositions 2 and 3 are false.
   D   Propositions 2 and 4 are false.

9 Complete the following statement.

   In conditions of perfect competition, the demand curve for the product of a firm:

   A   Is identical to the firm's marginal revenue curve
   B   Intersects the firm's marginal revenue curve at the point where MC = MR
   C   Intersects the firm's average cost
   D   Is perfectly inelastic

10 Which *one* of the following statements is incorrect?

   A   Investment in surplus capacity is a way in which a monopoly firm can try to deter other firms from entering the market.
   B   A natural monopoly is a market in which economies of scale are achievable up to a very high level of output.
   C   Predatory pricing is one method by which firms seek to enter a market which is dominated by a monopoly form or a few oligopolies.
   D   A contestable market is one in which sunk costs are low, so that the costs of entry and exit for predator firms are low.

Questions: The market system and the competitive process

11 Which *one* of the following statements about price discrimination is incorrect?

   A   Charging a different rate for telephone calls according to the time of day is price discrimination.

   B   Price discrimination might occur for reasons associated with differences in production costs between two or more markets.

   C   Price discrimination between two markets might be achieved because of transportation costs between the markets.

   D   Price discrimination can be achieved by separating markets on the basis of geography, age, time or consumers' ignorance.

12 All of the following are factor incomes except which *one*?

   A   Commission charges earned by an insurance salesman
   B   Dividends received from shares
   C   Cash paid to a window cleaner
   D   The pension earned by an ex-army officer now working for a security firm

13 According to the traditional theory of the firm, the equilibrium position for all firms will be where:

   A   Profits are maximised
   B   Output is maximised
   C   Revenue is maximised
   D   Costs are minimised

14 The law of diminishing returns can apply to a business only when:

   A   All factors of production can be varied.
   B   At least one factor of production is fixed.
   C   All factors of production are fixed.
   D   Capital used in production is fixed.

15 Which of the following statements about normal profit are correct?

   (i)   It is the reward for risk taking.
   (ii) It is the return to entrepreneurship.
   (iii) It is the cost of entrepreneurship.
   (iv) It is earned only in the short run.

   A   (i) and (ii) only
   B   (ii) and (iii) only
   C   (i), (ii) and (iii) only
   D   (i), (ii) and (iv) only

16 Consider the price and demand for Channel crossing tickets by sea ferry. The price of Channel crossings by hovercraft goes up. Which of the following would you expect to happen?

   A   The demand curve for sea ferry tickets will shift to the left, and their price will go down. More sea ferry tickets will be sold.

   B   The demand curve for sea ferry tickets will shift to the right, and their price will go up. More ferry tickets will be sold.

   C   The demand curve for sea ferry tickets will shift to the right and their price will go down. More sea ferry tickets will be sold.

   D   The demand curve for sea ferry tickets will shift to the right and their price will go up. Fewer sea ferry tickets will be sold.

17

Questions: The market system and the competitive process

17 Which of the following factors influence the elasticity of supply of a good?

1   The time period over which changes in supply are measured
2   The marginal cost of producing the good
3   The range of alternative production opportunities available to suppliers

A   Factors 1 and 2 only
B   Factors 1 and 3 only
C   Factors 1 and 3 only
D   Factors 1, 2 and 3

18 If the price elasticity of demand for petrol were zero, what would be the effect of an increase in taxation on petrol?

Effect

1   The consumer would pay all the tax.
2   The quantity of petrol consumed would be unchanged.
3   Total petrol sales would fall (in quantity) by the same proportion as the increase in price caused by the tax.
4   In order to maintain sales volume, petrol stations would have to adopt a pricing policy whereby they absorbed some of the tax.

A   Effect 1 only
B   Effects 1 and 2
C   Effects 2 and 3
D   Effect 4 only

19 A company sells two products, widgets and fidgets. Widgets have a high price elasticity of demand. Fidgets are relatively price inelastic. The company decides to spend £2 million on an advertising campaign for each product, in order to increase demand.

Which of the following statements would be true?

A   The supply curve of both products would shift to the right, and for widgets by a greater proportion than for fidgets.
B   The advertising campaign would be more successful for fidgets than for widgets.
C   The cost of the advertising campaign for fidgets could be covered by raising the price of the product.
D   The supply curve of both products would shift to the left, and for widgets by a greater proportionate amount than for fidgets.

20 Harold Ippoli employs 30 men in his factory which manufactures sweets and puddings. He pays them £5 per hour and they all work maximum hours. To employ one more man he would have to raise the wage rate to £5.50 per man hour. If all other costs remain constant, the marginal cost per hour of labour is now:

A   £20.50
B   £15.00
C   £5.50
D   £0.50

Questions: The market system and the competitive process   Notes

6 MULTIPLE CHOICE QUESTIONS

1 A firm's product has a price elasticity of demand equal to unity at all price levels. The current price for the product is P. Which of the following statements is/are correct?

   1   Marginal revenue equals zero.
   2   Average revenue is constant.
   3   Total revenue is at a maximum at the current price level.

   A   Statement 1 only is correct
   B   Statements 1 and 2 are correct
   C   Statements 3 only is correct
   D   Statements 1 and 3 are correct

2 In economics, what is the normal profit per unit of a product?

   A   The difference between its average revenue and average cost
   B   The difference between its marginal revenue and marginal cost
   C   An element in the cost of producing the product
   D   The profit per unit that should be earned under normal trading conditions

3 Locke and Boult Ltd is a firm of security guards which provides nightwatchmen to guard the premises of client firms. One such firm is Chinese Walls plc, which employs a guard from Locke and Boult for its head office building.

   1   The cost of the guard is a variable cost to Locke and Boult, since the number of guards the firm employs depends on the demand for their services.
   2   The cost of the guards is a fixed cost to Chinese Walls plc since the employment of the guard is not related to the volume of output of the firm.
   3   The cost of the guard is a social cost, since the guard protects the premises of Chinese Walls from burglary and fire.

   A   Statements 1 and 2 only are correct
   B   Statements 2 and 3 only are correct
   C   Statements 1 and 3 only are correct
   D   Statements 1, 2 and 3 are correct

4 Which of the following items could be the cause of diseconomies of scale?

   1   A firm has to lower its prices in order to sell a higher volume of output, and so producing more becomes unprofitable.
   2   Expansion of the industry as a whole forces up the cost of production resources for firms in the industry.
   3   Employees feel a growing sense of alienation and loss of motivation as their firm gets bigger.

   A   Items 1 and 2 only
   B   Items 2 and 3 only
   C   Items 1 and 3 only
   D   Item 3 only

Questions: The market system and the competitive process

5   For a profit-maximising firm in conditions of perfect competition, which of the following equations will be true in long run equilibrium?

   Equation
   1   Average Cost = Average Revenue
   2   Marginal Cost = Average Revenue
   A   Neither equation is correct
   B   Equation 1 only is correct
   C   Equation 2 only is correct
   D   Equations 1 and 2 are both correct

6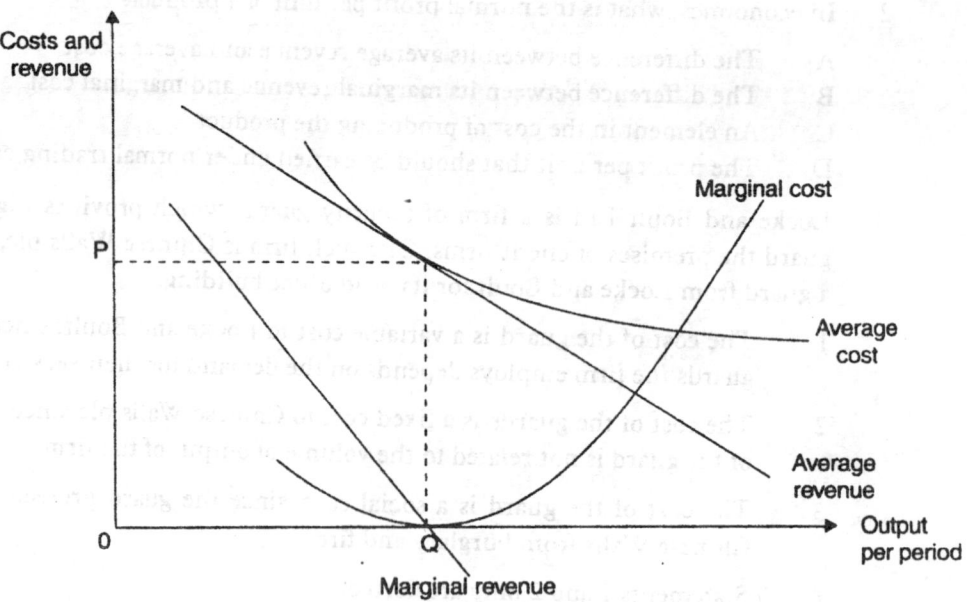

   The diagram above shows the cost curves and revenue curves for Hans Tordam Ltd, a firm of tulip growers. Which of the following statements is true?

   Statement
   1   Price P and output Q are the profit-maximising price and output levels for the firm.
   2   Price P and output Q are price and output levels at which the firm makes normal profits.
   3   Price P and output Q are the revenue-maximising price and output levels.
   A   Statement 1 only is correct
   B   Statements 1 and 2 are correct
   C   Statements 2 and 3 are correct
   D   Statements 1, 2 and 3 are correct

7   Which of the following statements best describes long run equilibrium in a market where there is monopolistic competition?
   A   Marginal revenue equals average cost.
   B   There is excess capacity in the industry since firms could reduce average costs by expanding output.
   C   Firms will earn supernormal profits because price exceeds marginal cost.
   D   Price equals marginal cost, but does not equal average cost.

Questions: The market system and the competitive process

8 Which one of the following statements about price discrimination is incorrect?

- A Dumping is a form of price discrimination.
- B For price discrimination to be possible, the seller must be able to control the supply of the product.
- C Price discrimination is only profitable where the elasticity of demand is different in at least two of the markets.
- D An example of price discrimination is the sale of first class and second class tickets on an aeroplane journey.

9 Muscles Ltd can only sell more of its product at progressively lower prices. Assuming that there is diminishing marginal physical productivity of labour, what implications does this have for the marginal revenue product curve (MRP curve) for the firm's labour?

- A The MRP curve will be completely inelastic.
- B The MRP curve will equal the average revenue product curve.
- C The MRP curve will fall faster than for a perfectly competitive firm.
- D The MRP curve will no longer be an indicator of wage levels.

10 The supply of skilled basketweavers is inelastic but not *perfectly* inelastic. There is an improvement in the productivity of basketweavers. Which of the following would you now expect to happen?

- A The number of basketweavers in employment will go down, but their wages will go up
- B The number in employment will be unchanged, and their wages will go up
- C The number in employment will go up, and their wages will go up
- D The number in employment will go up, but their wages will go down

11 Muddy Waters Ltd is an industrial company which has altered its production methods so that it has reduced the amount of waste discharged from its factory into the local river. Which of the following is most likely to be reduced?

- A Total private costs
- B Social cost
- C External benefit
- D Variable costs

12 Decreasing returns to scale only apply:

- A In the short run
- B In the long run
- C If there is one fixed factor of production
- D If companies have monopoly power

13 When only a small proportion of a consumer's income is spent on a good:

- A The demand for the good will be highly price elastic
- B The good is described as 'inferior'
- C A rise in the price of the good will strongly encourage a search for substitutes
- D The demand for the good will be price inelastic

Questions: The market system and the competitive process

14 The conditions necessary for a successful policy of price discrimination by a company include which of the following?

   (i)   There are at least two separate markets
   (ii) Marginal costs are different in each market
   (iii) The price elasticities of demand are different in each market
   (iv) The price elasticities of demand are the same in each market

   A   (i) and (ii) only
   B   (i) and (iii) only
   C   (i), (ii) and (iii) only
   D   (ii) and (iv) only

15 If the demand for a good is price inelastic, which *one* of the following statements is correct?

   A   If the price of the good rises, the total revenue earned by the producer increases.
   B   If the price of the good rises, the total revenue earned by the producer falls.
   C   If the price of the good falls, the total revenue earned by the producer increases.
   D   If the price of the good falls, the total revenue earned by the producer is unaffected.

16 The price elasticity of demand for a product = 1.
    The current selling price per unit is $30.
    The marginal cost of producing an extra unit would be $25.
    The average cost of production is currently $22.

    What would be the effect on total profits of producing and selling one extra unit?

   A $5 profit
   B $8 profit
   C $17 loss
   D $25 loss

17 Large firms can benefit from economies of scale, and gain a cost advantage over smaller competitor firms. In spite of this, small firms in industry manage to survive, and there are several reasons for this.

    Which of the following is *not* a reason for the survival of the small firm?

   A   The minimum efficient scale of production is at a relatively low level of output.
   B   Large firms suffer from diminishing returns at higher volumes of output.
   C   Small firms are able to fragment the market through product differentiation.
   D   Large firms are often bureaucratic and inefficient.

18 Suppose that all inputs are increased by 50%, and as a result, total output increases by 30%.

    This would be an illustration of which of the following?

    1   The law of variable proportions
    2   Decreasing returns to scale
    3   A rising long run average cost curve

   A   1 and 2 only
   B   2 and 3 only
   C   1 and 3 only
   D   2 only

Questions: The market system and the competitive process

19 Arguments for allocating resources through the market mechanism rather than through government direction include three of the following.

Which *one* is the exception?

- A It provides a more efficient means of communicating consumer wants to producers.
- B It ensures a fairer distribution of income.
- C It gives more incentive to producers to reduce costs.
- D It encourages companies to respond to consumer demand.

20 Which *one* of the following will tend to increase competition within an industry?

- A Economies of scale
- B Barriers to entry
- C Low fixed costs
- D Limited consumer knowledge

Questions: The market system and the competitive process

7 MULTIPLE CHOICE QUESTIONS

1 Which *one* of the following would be a variable cost to a firm?

    A   Mortgage payments on the factory
    B   The cost of raw materials
    C   Depreciation of machines owing to age
    D   Interest on debentures

2 The supply curve of labour will be more elastic:

    A   The more training is required for the job
    B   The greater is the immobility of labour between occupations
    C   For a single firm than for the industry as a whole
    D   The higher is the wage

3 Which *one* of the following would *not* act as a barrier to the entry of new firms into an industry?

    A   Perfect consumer knowledge
    B   Economies of scale
    C   High fixed costs of production
    D   Brand loyalty

4 The summer demand for hotel accommodation in London comes mainly from foreign tourists. Demand for hotel rooms in London in summer could be reduced by a fall in the price or value of which of the following?

    1   US dollars
    2   Aeroplane tickets
    3   Sterling

    A   Item 1 only
    B   Items 1 and 2 only
    C   Items 2 and 3 only
    D   Item 3 only

5 Which of the following changes will cause the demand curve for chocolate to shift to the left?

    1   A fall in the price of chocolate
    2   A health campaign which claims that chocolate makes you fat
    3   A rise in the price of chocolate substitutes
    4   A fall in consumers' income

    A   Change 1 only
    B   Changes 2 and 3 only
    C   Changes 2 and 4 only
    D   Changes 3 and 4 only

Questions: The market system and the competitive process

6 Suppose that, in a certain advanced industrialised country, the government has applied price controls over rents of both public and private rented accommodation for a number of years, and a serious problem of widespread homelessness has built up. Just recently, the rent price controls have been eased. Which of the following consequences should now occur?

1 An increase in homelessness
2 In the longer term, an increase in new building work
3 The provision of more rented accommodation
4 Fewer owner-occupied dwellings

A Consequences 1 and 2
B Consequences 2 and 3
C Consequences 3 and 4
D Consequences 1 and 4

7 The current price of lawnmowers is P. The supply of lawnmowers is inelastic in the short run, but more elastic in the longer run. The demand for lawnmowers falls. What would you expect to happen?

A In the short term the price will fall quite sharply, but in the longer term, the price will rise a little as supply is reduced, but will be less than P.
B In the short term the price will be unchanged, but in the longer term, the new equilibrium will be at a lower output quantity and a price less than P.
C In the short term the price will fall quite sharply, but in the longer term supply will be reduced so that the price rises above P.
D In the short term, the price will be unchanged, but in the longer term the new equilibrium will be at a lower output quantity and a price higher than P.

8 Smudge Paints plc and Dogsbrush plc are leading manufacturers of industrial paints, and their products compete with each other in the market. Which of the following statements would you expect to be correct?

A The products of Smudge Paints and Dogsbrush have a low positive cross elasticity of demand.
B The products of Smudge Paints and Dogsbrush have a low negative cross elasticity of demand.
C The products of Smudge Paints and Dogsbrush have high positive cross elasticity of demand.
D The products of Smudge Paints and Dogsbrush have a high negative cross elasticity of demand.

9 The purpose of a cartel is to:

A Rationalise production
B Reduce consumer uncertainty
C Standardise product quality
D Ensure that a dominant group of producers charge the same price

10 Which one of the following statements is incorrect?

A If the variable cost per unit is constant, a firm would minimise its short-run average cost by producing at maximum capacity.
B All fixed costs will be incurred in the short run, even if the firm were to shut down.
C Average variable cost per unit is another expression for marginal cost.
D When the marginal cost of producing a unit is equal to the marginal revenue from selling it, the firm will make a profit from the unit.

25

Questions: The market system and the competitive process

11 The law of diminishing marginal returns states that:

   A   As more factors of production are employed, output will rise initially and then fall

   B   As more factors of production are employed, output will rise, but at a diminishing rate

   C   As more variable factors of production are added to a fixed factor, output will rise at a faster rate initially and then fall

   D   As more variable factors of production are added to a fixed factor, output will rise at a decreasing rate after a certain point

12 The Hoppaboard Bus Company has just replaced its original fleet of four buses, each of which had a crew of two, with four new one-man buses. The new buses have the same capacity as the old buses. As a consequence, the company has been able to reduce the cost per passenger-mile and run the same service as before. This is because the company has obtained the benefits of:

   A   Economies of scale
   B   The division of labour
   C   Higher labour productivity
   D   Lower maintenance costs

13 A firm that is technically efficient is one which:

   A   Uses up-to-date machinery
   B   Produces a given quantity of output with minimum quantity of inputs
   C   Produces a given quantity of output with the least-cost mix of inputs
   D   Substitutes machinery in place of labour to improve output quantities

14 In the tin mining industry, the demand for tin miners will be less elastic:

   A   The more elastic the demand for tin
   B   The lower the proportion of miners' labour costs in the form's total costs
   C   The easier it is to substitute mining equipment for miners' labour
   D   The more difficult it is for firms to pass on higher wages cost in a higher price for tin

15 All of the following will result in a leftward shift in the supply curve of professional scientists *except*:

   A   A reduction in government spending on science education
   B   A fall in the real wage levels of professional scientists
   C   An increase in salaries being paid to science graduates in non-scientific jobs in commerce
   D   A longer period of pre-qualification training for scientists

16 Which *one* of the following statements is incorrect?

   A   If the effect of privatisation is to increase competition, the effect might be to reduce or eliminate allocative inefficiency.
   B   Privatisation means selling off nationalised industries by the government to the private sector.
   C   The effect of denationalisation could be to make firms more cost-conscious, because they will be under the scrutiny of stock market investors.
   D   The government might appoint consumer watchdogs to regulate privatised industries.

Questions: The market system and the competitive process

17 Economies of scale:

- A Can be gained only by monopoly firms
- B Are possible only if there is a sufficient demand for the product
- C Do not necessarily reduce unit costs of production
- D Depend on the efficiency of management

18 In response to an increase in demand for its product, Twisten Sheik Ltd starts an extra production shift at its factory, using existing plant and machinery. As a result, the firm's total output increases by 40%, but its total costs rise by 50%. The firm is experiencing:

- A Falling profit
- B An increase in average fixed cost
- C Decreasing returns to scale
- D Diminishing returns

19 ATC = Average total cost
AVC = Average variable cost
MC = Marginal cost

Which of the following statements is correct?

- A MC will equal ATC when ATC is at its minimum amount, but will not equal AVC when AVC is at its minimum.
- B MC will equal AVC when AVC is at its minimum amount, but will not equal ATC when ATC is at its minimum.
- C MC will equal ATC when ATC is at its minimum amount and AVC when AVC is at its minimum, which is at the same output level.
- D MC will equal ATC when ATC is at its minimum amount and AVC when AVC is at its minimum, but this will occur at different output levels.

20 Which of the following statements is incorrect?

- A When price elasticity of demand is 1 along the entire demand curve, total consumer expenditure on the product will be the same at all price levels.
- B If the quantity demanded of a product falls by 18% when its price is raised by 12%, demand is relatively price elastic.
- C When demand is price elastic, consumers' expenditure on a product will go up when its price is reduced.
- D Products which are staple goods or necessities of life have a low negative income elasticity of demand.

27

8 MULTIPLE CHOICE QUESTIONS

1 Demand for goods and services is known as derived demand when the purchasers are:

   A   Firms
   B   Households
   C   Both of the above
   D   Neither of the above

2 The satisfaction a person obtains from consuming one additional unit of a good is called its:

   A   Opportunity cost
   B   Marginal cost
   C   Economic rent
   D   Marginal utility

3 Which of the following goods have demand curves that do not slope downwards from left to right?

   A   A Giffen good
   B   An ostentation good
   C   A good for which demand is perfectly inelastic
   D   All of the above

4 The main factor affecting price elasticity of demand is:

   A   Availability of substitutes
   B   Availability of complements
   C   Percentage change in household income
   D   Existence of stocks of the good

5 An inferior good is a good for which demand:

   A   Is highly elastic
   B   Is dependent on fashion
   C   Falls as income rises
   D   Falls as the price of substitutes falls

6 A shift in the demand curve for a good cannot be caused by:

   A   A change in fashion
   B   A permanent fall in price
   C   An expected rise in the price of the good
   D   A fall in the price of complements

7 A rightward shift of the market supply curve for a manufactured good *cannot* be the result of:

   A   A fall in the cost of factors of production
   B   A rise in the price of substitutes in supply
   C   A rise in production efficiency
   D   Any of the above (A, B and C)

8 The price at which the volume of a good supplied in a market is equal to the volume that is demanded is called:

   A   The economic price
   B   The equilibrium price
   C   The equalising price
   D   The expected price

Questions: The market system and the competitive process

9 The price at which the volume of a good supplied is equal to the volume demanded is called:

   A   The market signalling price
   B   The market rewarding price
   C   The market clearing price
   D   The market exchanging price

10 Producer surplus exists when:

   A   A factor of production would earn less in an alternative use
   B   Some suppliers would be prepared to supply at less than the market price
   C   Supernormal profits are available in the short run
   D   The producer is a price maker

11 Which of the following is not a likely consequence of a government setting a maximum price that is lower than the equilibrium price?

   A   Waiting lists
   B   A black market
   C   An excess of supply over demand
   D   Rationing

12 When demand for a good is price elastic, a price increase will result in:

   A   A fall in demand but total revenue will rise
   B   A fall in demand and total revenue will fall
   C   A fall in demand and total revenue will remain the same
   D   None of the above (A, B and C)

13 If total revenue falls when price is reduced, then:

   A   The good in question is an inferior good
   B   Cross-elasticity of demand is positive
   C   Demand is switching to substitutes
   D   Demand is price-inelastic

14 Supply of a good is likely to be elastic if:

   A   The good is imperishable
   B   Barriers to entry to the industry are low
   C   Unemployment is low
   D   More than one of the above (A, B and C) is true

15 Which of the following is not a theoretical argument in favour of free markets under perfect competition?

   A   Producers will shift resources to their most efficient use in response to changing prices
   B   Merit goods are provided at the correct level of output
   C   The balance of supply and demand means that surpluses and shortages do not arise
   D   Consumers have maximum choice about how to spend their disposable income

Notes   **Questions: The market system and the competitive process**

16 An externality is:

   A   A good whose consumption by one person does not significantly reduce the amount available for others to consume

   B   A government intervention in an otherwise free market

   C   A consequence of an economic transaction that affects people not party to the transaction

   D   A private benefit arising from a public transaction

17 In a particular country, 75% of households buy their own homes, raising the mortgage finance to pay for them from finance companies. The interest rate on mortgage finance goes up from 10% to 12% annually. The interest rate elasticity of demand for mortgage finance is greater than 1 (ie is elastic). Which of the following consequences will occur?

   A   Total mortgage borrowing will go up and house prices will rise.
   B   Total mortgage borrowing will go up and house prices will fall.
   C   Total mortgage borrowing will fall and house prices will rise.
   D   Total mortgage borrowing will fall and house prices will fall.

18 If total receipts of the Dencom Telephone Company remain unchanged after it has put up its prices, which of the following would correctly describe demand in this case?

   A   It is absolutely inelastic.
   B   It is elastic.
   C   It has unitary elasticity.
   D   It is inelastic.

19 A manufacturer of power drills was charging £26 for a drill, and demand was 1,800 drills per week. He then raised the price to £30, and demand went down by 300 drills per week. What is the arc elasticity of demand between the prices of £26 and £30?

   A   0.79
   B   1.08
   C   1.25
   D   1.27

20 If the price elasticity of demand for luxury yachts were equal to zero, what would be the effect of an increase in taxation on the sale of luxury yachts?

   A   In order to maintain sales, yacht builders would have to adopt a pricing policy whereby they absorbed some of the tax.

   B   The purchasers of luxury yachts would pay all the extra tax in the form of a direct addition to the purchase price.

   C   Total sales of luxury yachts would fall by the same proportion as the increase in price caused by the higher tax.

   D   Some yacht builders would begin to incur losses because they could not pass on the full tax to the customer in the form of a higher price, and so would go out of business.

9 OBJECTIVE TEST QUESTIONS

1. A normal demand curve slopes downward from left to right

   ☐ True

   ☐ False

2. Complete the sentence below.

   An increase in demand for a good is likely to cause ▓▓▓▓▓▓▓▓ in demand for another good that is a substitute.

3. Complete the sentence below.

   An increase in demand for a good is likely to cause ▓▓▓▓▓▓▓▓ in demand for another good that is a complement.

4. A rise in household income is likely to result in a leftward shift in demand for inferior goods.

   ☐ True

   ☐ False

5. Annual demand for good A is 10 million units at £2.50 each and 8 million at £3.50 each. Is demand elastic or inelastic?

   ☐ Elastic

   ☐ Inelastic

6. Complete the sentence below.

   When demand is elastic an increase in price will result in a ▓▓▓▓▓▓▓▓ in total expenditure.

7. The defining characteristic of a Giffen good is that when price increases, demand falls.

   ☐ True

   ☐ False

8. Complete the following sentence.

   If the cross elasticity of demand for two goods is positive, the goods are ▓▓▓▓▓▓▓▓.

9. A supply curve with unit elasticity along all of its length is a straight line through the origin.

   ☐ True

   ☐ False

10. One of the causes of market imperfection is divergence between private costs and social costs.

    ☐ True

    ☐ False

Questions: The market system and the competitive process

11 Complete the sentence below.

When a transaction has an effect that extends beyond the parties to the transaction, that effect is called ....

12 The diagram below illustrates the effect of an indirect tax on the supplier and the consumer of a good. The total amount of the tax is the distance AB. Which part of this is paid by the consumer of the good?

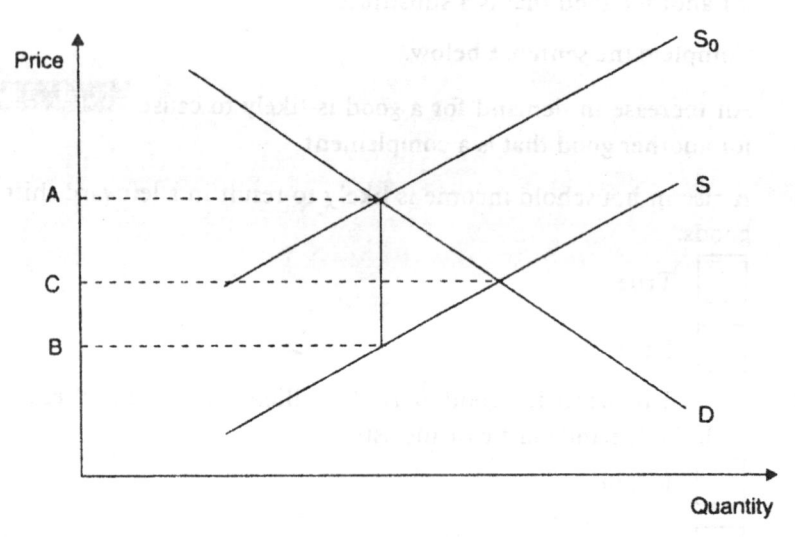

☐ AC

☐ CB

13 Complete the sentence below.

The demand by firms for goods is derived demand since it depends on .... for the goods those firms produce in turn.

14 Complements are goods that tend to be bought and used instead of one another.

☐ True

☐ False

15 Identify from the list below the events that would cause:

A A leftward shift in the demand curve
B A righthand shift in the demand curve

Insert A or B

☐ 1 A rise in household income

☐ 2 A rise in the price of substitutes

☐ 3 A rise in the price of complements

☐ 4 A forecast rise in the price of the good

16 A leftward shift in the supply curve will occur if there is a rise in the price of other goods.

☐ True

☐ False

Questions: The market system and the competitive process

17 Complete the sentence below.

Some purchasers would be prepared to pay more than the equilibrium price for a good. The extra amount they would be prepared to pay is called ....

18 A legal minimum price is set which is below the equilibrium. What will be the magnitude of the eventual excess supply?

19 Strike out the word which does apply in the sentence below.

When price is increased and there is zero change in demand, demand is perfectly **elastic/inelastic**.

20 The time horizon is one of the principal factors affecting the elasticity of both supply and demand. Is demand likely to be more elastic the longer the timescale or less elastic?

☐ More

☐ Less

Questions: The market system and the competitive process

10 OBJECTIVE TEST QUESTIONS

1. What is the name of the function identified as X in the diagram below?

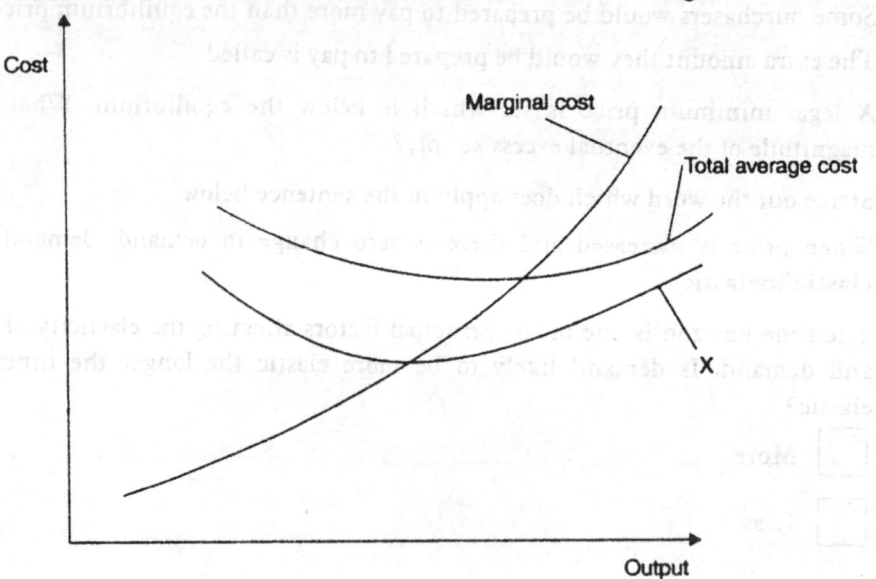

    (Diagram: Cost vs Output curves labelled "Marginal cost", "Total average cost", with point X on the average cost curve.)

2. Delete the incorrect words from the sentence below.

    When the average cost curve is falling, marginal cost will be **below/above/equal to** it.

3. Between 1815 and 1832 MacDonald's Farm remained the same in size but employed varying numbers of people on the cultivation of grain. The weather was the same each year, but the output varied.

    What economic principle is illustrated by the figures given below?

Workers	Output (bushels)
1	270
2	300
3	310
4	314
5	316

    _____ (write your answer here)

Questions: The market system and the competitive process

4 The diagram below shows average revenue and marginal revenue for a price maker. Which is which?

☐ A is marginal revenue, B is average revenue

☐ A is average revenue, B is marginal revenue

5 Complete the following sentence.

At the output level where marginal cost is equal to marginal revenue, profit is ....

6 Economies of scale cause average cost to decline in the short run.

☐ True

☐ False

7 A legal minimum wage can increase numbers employed in some industries.

☐ True

☐ False

8 Complete the following sentence.

The elasticity of demand for labour in an industry will reflect the .... of the end product.

9 The secondary sector of the economy consists of industries that provide services.

☐ True

☐ False

10 Complete the following sentence.

One of the conditions that must apply if perfect competition is to exist is that the products of all the firms in a market must be ....

35

Notes   **Questions: The market system and the competitive process**

11 Strike out the **words** that are incorrect in the statement below.

   The diagram shows a firm operating in a perfectly competitive market. The shaded area ABCD represents **abnormal profit/short term loss**.

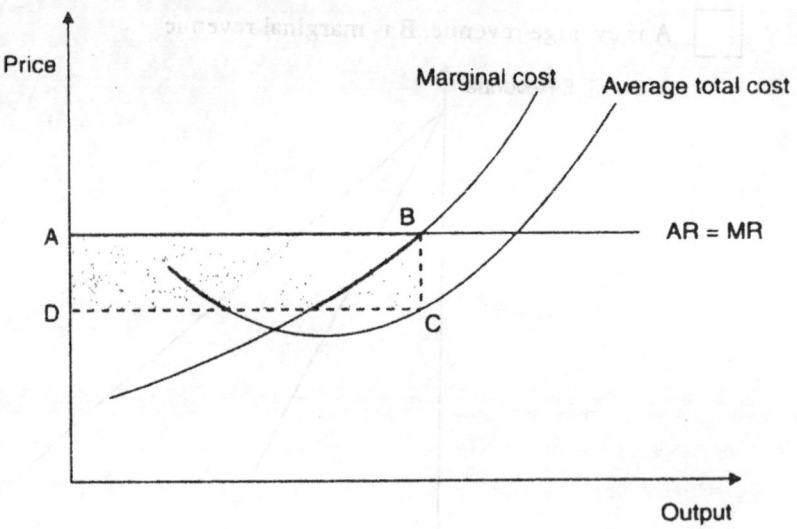

12 A perfectly competitive firm will be in equilibrium when price is equal to marginal cost.

   ☐ True

   ☐ False

13 Complete the following sentence.

   A monopolist will maximise its sales revenue when its marginal revenue is equal to ....

14 Elasticity of demand does not affect a monopolist's ability to operate a policy of price discrimination between markets.

   ☐ True

   ☐ False

15 A firm operating under conditions of monopolistic competition is a price taker.

   ☐ True

   ☐ False

16 Complete the sentence below.

   Oligopoly differs from perfect competition in that the product is .... but there are .... firms in the market.

17 Complete the following sentence.

   The kinked demand curve model of oligopoly features a discontinuous .... revenue curve.

18 Complete this sentence.

   Monopoly erodes the consumer surplus that would exist under perfect competition. The element of consumer surplus that is totally eliminated is called the .... due to monopoly.

Questions: The market system and the competitive process   Notes

19   It is possible for the average total cost curve to be falling while the average variable cost curve is rising.

☐ True

☐ False

20   Complete the following sentence.

Economies of scale that affect a whole industry are called .... economies of scale.

Notes **Questions: The macroeconomic framework**

THE MACROECONOMIC FRAMEWORK

The sets of questions 11 to 16 cover the macroeconomic framework, the subject of Part C of the BPP Study Text for Paper 3a.

---

11 MULTIPLE CHOICE QUESTIONS

1 Which *one* of the following is *not* a function of a central bank?

   A   The conduct of fiscal policy
   B   Management of the national debt
   C   Holder of the foreign exchange reserves
   D   Lender of the last resort

2 The current account of the balance of payments includes all the following items except which one?

   A   The inflow of capital investment by multinational companies
   B   Exports of manufactured goods
   C   Interest payments on overseas debts
   D   Expenditure in the country by overseas visitors

3 Which of the following would lead to a rise in the demand for money?

   (i)   A rise in disposable income
   (ii) A fall in interest rates
   (iii) An expectation of falling share prices
   (iv) A decrease in the money supply

   A   (i) and (ii) only
   B   (ii) and (iii) only
   C   (ii), (iii) and (iv) only
   D   (i), (ii) and (iii) only

4 Which *one* of the following would appear as a liability in a clearing bank's balance sheet?

   A   Advances to customers
   B   Money at call and short notice
   C   Customers' deposit accounts
   D   Discounted bills

5 Other things being equal, all of the following would lead to a rise in share prices except which one?

   A   A rise in interest rates
   B   A reduction in corporation tax
   C   A rise in company profits
   D   A decline in the number of new share issues

6 Which *one* of the following is *most likely* to result from an increase in the size of the public sector net cash requirement?

   A   A decrease in the rate of inflation
   B   A reduction in the level of taxation
   C   A rise in the price of shares
   D   A rise in rates of interest

Questions: The macroeconomic framework

7 Venture capital is best described as:

    A   Investment funds provided for established companies
    B   Short-term investment in eurocurrency markets
    C   Capital funds that are highly mobile between financial centres
    D   Equity finance in high-risk enterprises

8 Which *one* of the following would cause a fall in the level of aggregate demand in an economy?

    A   A decrease in the level of imports
    B   A fall in the propensity to save
    C   A decrease in government expenditure
    D   A decrease in the level of income tax

9 Structural unemployment is best defined as that caused by:

    A   The long-term decline of particular industries
    B   The trade cycle
    C   An insufficient level of aggregate demand
    D   Seasonal variations in demand for particular goods and services

10 The real rate of interest is:

    A   The rate at which the central bank lends to financial institutions
    B   The bank base rate
    C   The difference between the money rate of interest and the rate of inflation
    D   The annualised percentage rate of interest

11 GNP (Gross National Product) at factor cost may be best defined as:

    A   The total of goods and services produced within an economy over a given period of time.
    B   The total expenditure of consumers on domestically produced goods and services.
    C   All incomes received by residents in a country in return for factor services provided domestically and abroad.
    D   The value of total output produced domestically plus net property income from abroad, minus capital consumption.

12 Which **one** of the following can be used by governments to finance a public sector net cash requirement?

    A   A rise in direct taxation
    B   The sale of public assets
    C   An increase in interest rates
    D   An issue of government savings certificates

13 A progressive tax is one where the tax payment:

    A   Rises as income increases
    B   Falls as income increases
    C   Is a constant proportion of income
    D   Rises at a faster rate than income increases

Questions: The macroeconomic framework

14 All of the following macroeconomic policies would lead to a fall in unemployment *except* which *one*?

  A A devaluation of the currency
  B The introduction of a profit tax
  C A reduction in interest rates
  D An increase in import tariffs

15 All of the following will lead to a rise in the total of household incomes *except* which *one*?

  A A fall in the rate of saving
  B A rise in interest rates
  C An increase in the average level of rents
  D Increased profitability of business

16 Which of the following is *not* a function of money?

  A Storing wealth
  B Facilitating the operation of trade credit
  C Representing the value of goods
  D Permitting the operation of market forces

17 Which of the following is a liquid asset, that is, one that may readily be converted into cash without loss of face value?

  A Government stock
  B Shares in a bank
  C Old master paintings
  D Money market deposits

18 Which one of the following is *not* likely to increase the rate of interest a business borrower has to pay on a loan?

  A An extended period of credit
  B Moderate financial gearing
  C A project based on specially developed technology
  D A low level of physical assets

19 Which *one* of the following is *least* likely to influence the rate of interest a business is charged on a loan?

  A Existing levels of debt of the business
  B The rate of corporate tax paid by the business
  C The business's past trading record
  D The availability of assets to secure borrowings

20 'Maturity transformation' is a process associated with:

  A Insurance companies
  B Wine merchants
  C Keynes' theory of the money supply
  D Bills of exchange

12 MULTIPLE CHOICE QUESTIONS

1   Which *one* of the following would you expect to be included in 'broad money' but *not* in narrow money?

   A   Banks' till money
   B   Clearing banks' operational deposits with the central bank
   C   Banks' retail deposits
   D   Bank notes in circulation

2   The credit multiplier is the process by which:

   A   An injection of government spending increases national income
   B   The relationship between the value of a bank's deposits and its cash holdings is governed
   C   Cash leaks out of the banking system into less formal accumulations
   D   Government controls the creation of credit

3   Securitisation of debt means:

   A   Creating tradable securities that are backed by illiquid assets
   B   Creating a mortgage as security for a loan
   C   The issue of new government stocks to finance repayment of old ones that have reached maturity
   D   Purchase of trade debts at a discount

4   Which of the following is a central bank least likely to be responsible for?

   A   Fixing the general level of interest rates
   B   Regulating the banking industry
   C   Determining the public sector borrowing requirement
   D   Maintaining national reserves of foreign currency

5   Which *one* of the following is *not* fundamental to retail banking operations?

   A   Profitability
   B   Liquidity
   C   Security
   D   Elasticity

6   The paradox of thrift arises because:

   A   Banks are able to create credit
   B   The marginal propensity to save varies between households
   C   Some savings are held as cash
   D   With high levels of welfare benefits some people are better off unemployed than in work

7   In the theory of the demand for money, the transactions demand for money is determined by:

   A   The level of consumers' incomes
   B   Expected changes in interest rates
   C   Expected changes in bond prices
   D   The level of notes and coins in circulation

Questions: The macroeconomic framework

8 Which of the following are functions of a central bank?

    (i) Issuing notes and coins
    (ii) Supervision of the banking system
    (iii) Conducting fiscal policy on behalf of the government
    (iv) Holding foreign exchange reserves

    A (i), (ii) and (iii) only
    B (i), (ii) and (iv) only
    C (i), (iii) and (iv) only
    D (ii), (iii) and (iv) only

9 Which *one* of the following will result if a firm is taxed by an amount equal to the external costs that its productive activities impose on society?

    A Resource allocation will be improved since prices more closely reflect costs and benefits.
    B There will be a misallocation of resources because the price mechanism has been interfered with.
    C The increase in costs will lead the firm to raise output in order to maintain profits.
    D The firm will maintain output and profits by passing the costs of the tax on to its customers.

10 Keynes suggested that investment grows faster then consumption because of:

    A The multiplier
    B The J-curve effect
    C A low marginal propensity to consume
    D The accelerator

11 The trade cycle is:

    A The accounting reference period
    B A sequence of varying rates of growth
    C The period over which all factors of production may be varied
    D The process by which a small injection into the circular flow produces a larger rise in national income

12 To which *one* of the following statements would supply side economists subscribe?

    A Price regulation enhances the signalling function of market prices.
    B Government subsidies encourage inefficiency.
    C An unregulated labour market cannot ensure full employment.
    D An unregulated labour market encourages over-manning.

13 If there is a reduction in government spending, there will not necessarily be a fall in National Income if there is an increase in:

    1 Exports
    2 Taxation
    3 Investment

    A 1 and/or 2
    B 1 and/or 3
    C 2 and/or 3
    D Any or all of 1, 2 and 3

Questions: The macroeconomic framework

14 Which one of the following items is most likely to increase the circular flow of income?

    A   Increased taxation
    B   Increased spending on imports
    C   Lower government spending
    D   Reductions in personal savings

15 Net National Product at factor cost
+ Capital consumption
+ Indirect taxes on expenditure
− Subsidies
equals

    A   Gross National Product at market prices
    B   Gross National Product at factor cost
    C   Gross Domestic Product at market prices
    D   Gross Domestic Product at factor cost

16 Which of the following cannot be termed a 'transfer payment' for the purpose of National Income accounting?

    A   Interest paid to holders of government stock
    B   Salaries paid to Members of Parliament
    C   Payments of state pensions
    D   Social security payments

17 The marginal propensity to consume measures

    A   The relationship between changes in consumption and changes in consumer utility
    B   The proportion of household incomes spent on consumer goods
    C   The proportion of total national Income spent on consumer goods
    D   The relationship between changes in consumption and changes in income

18 Which of the following investments creates an injection into the circular flow of income?

    A   An increase by a firm in its stocks of finished goods, prior to a marketing campaign
    B   The purchase by a pension fund of shares in a newly privatised company
    C   The purchase of a second-hand piece of farming machinery with their savings by a farming co-operative group
    D   The takeover of one company by another company

19 Investment in a closed economy (with no government sector) is expected to increase by £6,000 million in the next year. Given a marginal propensity to save of 0.4, what will be the expected growth in national income?

    A   £10,000 million
    B   £15,000 million
    C   £125 million
    D   £133 million (approx)

20 *Statement* 1

An increase in saving will always act to the benefit of a country.

Statement 2

The paradox of thrift suggests that an attempt to increase the amount saved out of a given level of national income will result in a fall in national income.

A   Statement 1 is correct.
    Statement 2 is correct.

B   Statement 1 is correct.
    Statement 2 is incorrect.

C   Statement 1 is incorrect.
    Statement 2 is correct.

D   Statement 1 is incorrect.
    Statement 2 is incorrect.

13 MULTIPLE CHOICE QUESTIONS

1 The accelerator principle states:

   A How an initial increase in a component of national income leads to much greater eventual rise in national income

   B That a small change in investment will lead to a much greater change in the output of consumer goods

   C That a small change in the output of consumer goods will lead to a much greater change in the production of capital goods

   D That changes in investment level are the cause of trade cycles

2 Which of the following can indicate trade cycle movements?

   Item
   1 Raw material prices
   2 Gross Domestic Product
   3 Seasonal unemployment

   A Items 1 and 2 only
   B Items 2 and 3 only
   C Items 1 and 3 only
   D Items 1, 2 and 3

3 All of the following would tend to result in a reduction of the rate of growth in the broad money supply *except* which *one*?

   A An increase in the rate of interest offered on national Savings
   B A reduction in the Public Sector Net Cash Requirement
   C The sale of long-term bonds by the government to the banking sector
   D The sale of Treasury bills to private sector financial institutions

4 A financial intermediary is best defined as:

   A An institution that matches lenders' supply of funds with borrowers' demand for funds

   B An institution that operates on the Stock Exchange, matching buyers and sellers of stocks and shares

   C An institution that allows firms to obtain equipment from suppliers by providing leasing or hire purchase finance

   D An institution that acts as a buffer between the Bank of England and the rest of the UK banking system

5 Which of the following items will not be found in the assets of a retail bank?

   A Overdrafts
   B Bank bills
   C Customers' deposits
   D Loans to the money markets

6 The velocity of circulation can be defined as:

   A The money stock in a given period divided by the level of prices

   B The average time in which households spend their money income

   C The total value of transactions in a given time period divided by the average price level

   D The number of times in a given time period that a unit of money is used to purchase final output

Questions: The macroeconomic framework

7   According to Keynes, which one of the following is very sensitive to changes in interest rates?

   A   The money supply
   B   The speculative demand for money
   C   The precautionary demand for money
   D   The transactions demand for money

8   Which of the following actions by the government would be most likely to increase aggregate monetary demand?

   A   Reductions in subsidies on food, off-set by a reduction in taxation
   B   A rise in the Bank of England's short-term interest rate (for open market operations)
   C   Increased value added tax on a wide range of goods
   D   Insisting that public corporations should break even

9   Which of the following factors might cause cost-push inflation?

   Factor

   1   Higher wage levels in domestic industries
   2   Higher consumer spending
   3   Higher import prices

   A   Factor 1 only
   B   Factors 1 and 2 only
   C   Factors 1 and 3 only
   D   Factors 2 and 3 only

10   Frictional unemployment arises because of:

   A   Long-term changes in the pattern of demand
   B   A difficulty in speedily matching unemployed workers with jobs
   C   A deficiency of demand in the economy
   D   Certain industries regularly shedding labour at certain times of the year

11   Which *one* of the following measures would be most consistent with the views of Friedman and other monetarist economists, for reducing the rate of inflation or unemployment?

   A   The government should impose an incomes policy to keep inflation down.
   B   The government can achieve lower unemployment, but only by accepting high levels of inflation.
   C   The government should control the money supply so as to keep output in the economy at a full employment level.
   D   Lower unemployment can be achieved without higher inflation if the government reduces welfare benefits for the unemployed.

12   Howard earns £8,000 per year and pays £1,000 in income tax. Hugh earns £16,000 per year and pays £2,500 in income tax. Harold earns £24,000 per year and pays £5,500 in income tax. The income tax system is:

   A   Regressive
   B   Flat rate
   C   Proportional
   D   Progressive

13 Which *one* of the following items is *not* included in the calculation of Gross National Product at factor cost?

    A   The cost of building new government offices
    B   Value added tax on business services
    C   Dividends received from shares in a company abroad
    D   Imputed rent of owner-occupied houses

14 The following data relate to National Income statistics in Muvovia, which are compiled in the same way as in the UK.

	2001 Actual prices $ million	2002 Actual prices $ million
Consumers' expenditure	200,000	225,000
General government final consumption	70,000	74,000
Gross domestic fixed capital formation	54,000	60,000
Imports	92,000	99,000
Exports	93,000	94,000
Taxes on expenditure	52,000	50,000
Subsidies	8,000	10,000

    The general rate of inflation in Muvovia between 2001 and 2002 was 10%. The *real* change in Gross Domestic Product at market prices between 2001 and 2002, in percentage terms, was:

    A   A fall of about 1%
    B   A rise of about 1%
    C   A rise of about 2%
    D   A rise of about 2½%

15 Which *one* of the following statements is correct?

    A   Two countries with the same total National Income will have roughly the same living standards.
    B   Services provided free to the public, such as police work and state education, are valued at opportunity cost in the National Income statistics.
    C   Official statistics might over-estimate the National Income for a country with a strong black economy.
    D   Gross National Product figures are often used in preference to net National Product figures because of difficulty in calculating capital consumption.

16 An inflationary gap in the economy could be closed by an increase in the:

    A   Accelerator and multiplier
    B   Government's budget surplus
    C   Average propensity to consume
    D   Country's export surplus

17 The effect of the multiplier on national income will be small:

    A   When there is high unemployment in the economy
    B   When the marginal propensity to save is low
    C   Because of a deflationary gap
    D   Because of leakages from the circular flow in addition to savings

Notes   Questions: The macroeconomic framework

18 Which of the following is the correct sequence in a business cycle?

   A   Boom Recession Depression Recovery
   B   Recession Recovery Boom Depression
   C   Boom Recovery Recession Depression
   D   Recovery Recession Depression Boom

19 A banking system in a small country consists of just five banks. Each bank has decided to maintain a minimum cash ratio of 10%. Each bank now receives additional cash deposits of £1 million. There will now be a further increase in total bank deposits up to a maximum of:

   A   £500,000
   B   £5 million
   C   £45 million
   D   £50 million

20 If all the commercial banks in a national economy operated on a cash reserve ratio of 20%, how much cash would have to be deposited with the banks for the money supply to increase by £300 million?

   A   £60 million
   B   £75 million
   C   £225 million
   D   £240 million

14 MULTIPLE CHOICE QUESTIONS

1 Maturity transformation is:
   - A The process by which loans get closer to redemption as time passes
   - B The amount payable to redeem a loan or security at its maturity
   - C The way in which interest rates vary according to the duration of the loan
   - D The process by which short term deposits are re-lent by banks as longer term loans

2 If the real rate of interest is 3% pa and the expected rate of inflation is 6% pa, the nominal interest rate will be approximately:
   - A ½%
   - B 2%
   - C 3%
   - D 9%

3 For the Quantity Theory of Money equation MV = PT to explain short-run price behaviour, it is necessary that:
   - A P varies inversely with M
   - B Interest rates remain unchanged
   - C Changes in V in the short run are predictable
   - D T remains unchanged

4 Other things remaining the same, according to Keynes, an increase in the money supply will tend to reduce:
   - A Interest rates
   - B Liquidity preference
   - C The volume of bank overdrafts
   - D Prices and incomes

5 A government may seek to reduce the rate of demand-pull inflation by any of the following means *except*:
   - A Reducing interest rates
   - B Increasing value added tax
   - C Applying more stringent controls over bank lending
   - D Reducing public expenditure

6 The Keynesian view of inflation is associated with *which* of the following concepts?
   - A Rational expectations of inflation
   - B Supply side economics
   - C The natural rate of unemployment
   - D The inflationary gap

7 If a county's consumer price index changed from 250 to 260 over a period of twelve months, this would indicate that:
   - A The standard of living has fallen
   - B Wages will need to rise by 4% if incomes are to keep pace with price rises
   - C The pattern of consumer expenditure has probably changed during the year
   - D The value of money has fallen

49

Questions: The macroeconomic framework

8 Structural unemployment is best defined as unemployment caused by:

   A   Defects in the industrial and commercial structure
   B   A long-term decline in a particular industry
   C   A mismatch between available jobs and the unemployed
   D   A switch from labour-intensive to capital-intensive production methods

9 Which *one* of the following measures has *not* been recommended by Friedman and like-minded monetarist economists as a means of reducing the natural rate of unemployment to a lower level?

   A   Measures to stimulate consumer demand for more goods
   B   Schemes to retrain workers in new job skills
   C   Measures to cut trade union power
   D   Restructuring the income tax system

10 The government of a certain country decides to introduce a poll tax, which will involve a flat levy of £200 on every adult member of the population. This new tax could be described as:

   A   Regressive
   B   Proportional
   C   Progressive
   D   Ad valorem

11 If a reduction in the taxes on alcoholic drinks resulted in a less even distribution of wealth in society, with a greater proportion of wealth in the hands of the rich sections of society, we could conclude that, *on average*:

   A   People with low incomes spend more on alcoholic drinks than people with high incomes
   B   People with low incomes spend less on alcoholic drinks than people with high incomes
   C   People with low incomes spend a bigger proportion of their income on alcoholic drinks than people with high incomes
   D   People with low incomes spend a lower proportion of their income on alcoholic drinks than people with high incomes

12 The opportunity cost of leisure can be defined as the quantity of goods and services which individuals forgo by not working. This being so, the opportunity cost of leisure would fall as a consequence of:

   A   An increase in (wealth) tax on capital transfers
   B   A reduction in the rate of income tax
   C   An increase in the rate of indirect taxes
   D   Introducing a poll tax

13 All of the following measure might be used by a government to help to control cost-push inflation *except*:

   A   A revaluation/appreciation of the currency
   B   Higher direct taxation
   C   Measures to control 'wage drift'
   D   Linking public sector pay increases to productivity improvements

Questions: The macroeconomic framework

14 Which *one* of the following measures would be expected to reduce the level of unemployment?

    A   An increase in value added tax
    B   A higher budget surplus
    C   A reduction in employers' National Insurance contributions
    D   A reduction in investment in the nationalised industries

15 Which *one* of the following is an aspect of fiscal policy measures by the government?

    A   To raise short-term interest rates in the money markets
    B   To support the exchange rate for the country's currency
    C   To control growth in the money supply
    D   To alter rates of taxation

16 'Supply side' economics concerns:

    A   The behaviour of the microeconomic supply curve
    B   The supply of factors of production in response to changing levels of factor rewards
    C   The behaviour of the aggregate supply curve in connection with the levels of prices, incomes and employment
    D   The effect that an increase in the supply of money has on inflation

17 If a government wishes to increase consumer spending, it could increase the rate of:

    A   Income tax
    B   Corporation tax
    C   Import duties
    D   Social security payments

18 The recession phase of the trade cycle will normally be accompanied by all of the following *except* which *one*?

    A   A rise in the rate of inflation
    B   A fall in the level of national output
    C   An improvement in the trade balance
    D   A rise in the level of unemployment

19 All of the following will normally lead to a fall in the level of economic activity in an economy *except* which *one*?

    A   A rise in cyclical unemployment
    B   A fall in business investment
    C   A decrease in government expenditure
    D   A rise in interest rates

20 Which *one* of the following is *not* a part of the equity capital market?

    A   Pension funds
    B   Retail banks
    C   Life assurance companies
    D   Venture capital organisations

15 OBJECTIVE TEST QUESTIONS

1 Complete the sentence below.

   Unemployment caused by long-term changes in the conditions under which an industry operates is called ▓▓▓▓▓▓▓▓ unemployment.

2 Delete the incorrect words in the sentence below.

   Unemployment that rises and falls in a regular pattern not associated with the overall economic cycle is called **frictional/seasonal/cyclical** unemployment.

3 Keynesian demand management techniques are most appropriate for reducing structural unemployment.

   ☐ True

   ☐ False

4 Label the axes of the diagram of the Phillips curve below in the boxes provided.

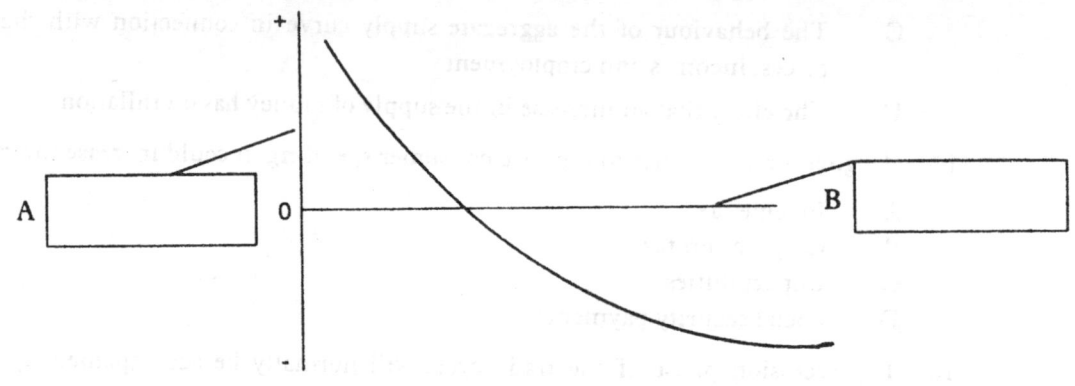

5 What is the five-letter abbreviation used to denote the unemployment rate associated with the long-run Phillips curve?

   ▓▓▓▓▓▓▓ (write your answer here)

6 If UK interest rates rise, UK exports will become cheaper.

   ☐ True

   ☐ False

7 Inflation caused by a persistent excess of aggregate demand over aggregate supply is called demand push inflation.

   ☐ True

   ☐ False

8 Using the new quantity theory of money identity MV ≡ PQ, if the velocity of circulation and level of national output remain constant but the money supply grows by 5%, what will happen to inflation?

9 Expectational inflation arises when governments raise interest rates and firms and households anticipate that prices will rise.

   ☐ True

   ☐ False

10 If interest rates rise, the market price of fixed interest investments such as bonds will fall.

☐ True

☐ False

11 The multiplier principle explains how investment in capital goods responds disproportionately to changes in consumer demand.

☐ True

☐ False

12 Insert the missing term in the equation below.

GNP − GDP = _____

13 In Fitzrovia, the marginal propensity to consume is 0.8. The Fitzrovian government injects £4bn into the economy. What is the theoretical increase in national income that should ensue?

14 Delete the incorrect **bold** words in the sentence below.

Keynes argued that **an increase/ a decrease** in the money supply would lead to lower interest rates.

15 Which of the following is most likely to result from a government policy of high interest rates? (Tick all that apply.)

A ☐ Lower consumer demand

B ☐ Less overseas investment in the currency concerned

C ☐ Slower growth in the money supply

Notes   Questions: The macroeconomic framework

16   OBJECTIVE TEST QUESTIONS

1   Label the diagram below using the list of terms provided.

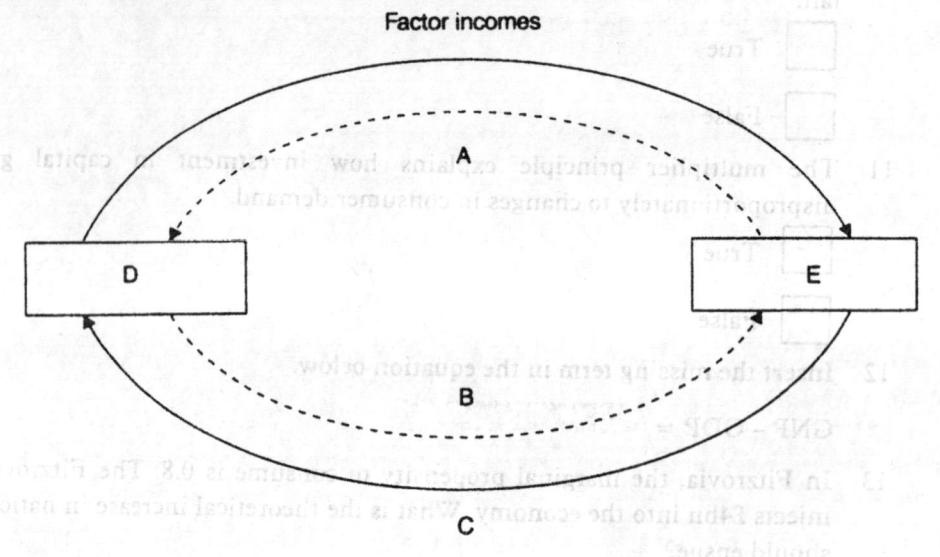

Factor incomes

(Diagram: circular flow with labels A at top, B at bottom, D on left box, E on right box, C at bottom)

1   Firms
2   Households
3   Factors of production
4   Goods and services
5   Expenditure on purchases

(4 marks)

2   Withdrawals from the circular flow consist of savings, taxation and exports.

☐ True

☐ False

3   Insert the missing term in the equation below.

GDP + ▓▓▓▓▓▓ = GNP

4   Insert the missing term in the equation below.

National income = GNP − ▓▓▓▓▓▓

5   Identify the full employment level of real national income on the diagram below.

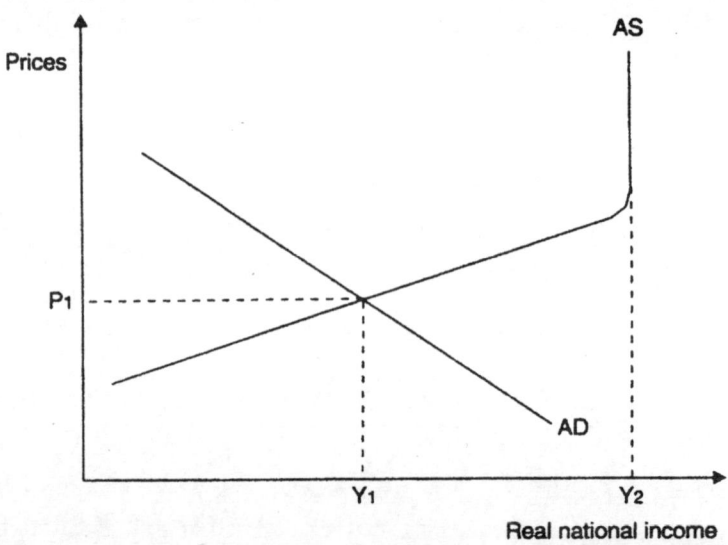

(Diagram: AD/AS diagram with Prices on vertical axis, Real national income on horizontal axis, equilibrium at P₁, Y₁, and Y₂ at the vertical part of AS)

54

☐ P₁

☐ Y₁

☐ Y₂

6 On the diagram below, does the distance P₁P₂ represent an inflationary gap or a deflationary gap?

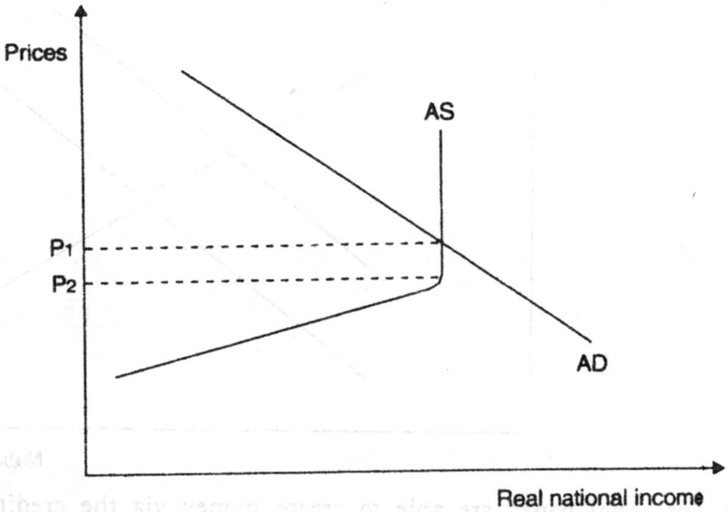

☐ Inflationary gap

☐ Deflationary gap

7 A redistribution of income from rich to poor households is likely to lead to an increase in aggregate demand.

☐ True

☐ False

8 In Dumnonia, the marginal propensity to consume is 0.9. The Dumnonian government injects £2bn into the economy. What is the theoretical increase in national income that should ensure?

9 The accelerator principle explains how capital investment changes in direct proportion to changes in consumption.

☐ True

☐ False

Questions: The macroeconomic framework

10 The diagram below shows how a price shock can lead to stagflation. Has the **aggregate supply** curve moved from left to right or from right to left?

☐ Left to right

☐ Right to left

11 Commercial banks are able to create money via the credit multiplier mechanism because they are required to hold adequate deposits with the central bank.

☐ True

☐ False

12 Government macroeconomic policy must take account of **automatic stabilisers**. These are of two types. One type is tax revenues that fall as national income rises.

☐ True

☐ False

13 What is the name given to the effect of the automatic stabilisers when the economy is recovering from a recession?

▓▓▓▓▓▓▓▓▓▓▓▓▓▓▓ (*write your answer here*)

14 VAT is a regressive tax.

☐ True

☐ False

15 The so-called 'poverty trap' exists because of the effect of regressive taxes.

☐ True

☐ False

16 The Phillips curve suggests that it may be possible to increase total tax revenue by reducing tax rates.

☐ True

☐ False

17 While inflation has its disadvantages, it also has the advantage of redistributing wealth from rich to poor.

☐ True

☐ False

18 Complete the sentence below.

Keynes suggested that people choose to keep money on hand in case they have a sudden need for it; this is called the ▆▆▆▆▆▆▆▆ motive.

19 Strike out the incorrect word from the sentence below.

Keynes argued that an increase in the money supply would lead to **higher/lower** interest rates.

20 According to the new quantity theory of money associated with *Friedman*, increases in the money supply will have a direct effect on aggregate demand.

☐ True

☐ False

Notes *Questions: The open economy*

THE OPEN ECONOMY

The sets of questions 17 to 20 cover the open economy, the subject of Part D of the BPP Study Text for Paper 3a.

---

17 MULTIPLE CHOICE QUESTIONS

1   The main advantage of a system of flexible (floating) exchange rates is that it:

   A   Provides certainty for international traders
   B   Provides automatic correction of balance of payments deficits
   C   Reduces international transactions costs
   D   Provides policy discipline for governments

2   The comparative cost model of international trade shows that trade arises because of differences between countries in:

   A   The absolute costs of production
   B   Patterns of consumer demand
   C   The opportunity costs of production
   D   The structure of production

3   A restriction imposed on the flow of imports into a country would be expected to lead to all of the following *except* which one?

   A   An improvement in the trade balance
   B   A reduction in unemployment
   C   Reduced competition for domestic producers
   D   A fall in the rate of inflation

4   A fixed exchange rate is unlikely to be put under pressure by:

   A   Capital movements
   B   Trade in goods and services
   C   Falling unemployment
   D   Speculation

5   The theory of comparative advantage suggests that countries should:

   A   Diversify their production as much as possible
   B   Engage in trade if the opportunity costs of production differ between countries
   C   Engage in trade only if each country has an absolute advantage in at least one good or service
   D   Aim to make their economies self-sufficient

6   Which one of the following is not a benefit from countries forming a monetary union and adopting a single currency?

   A   International transaction costs are reduced
   B   Exchange rate uncertainly is removed
   C   It economies on foreign exchange reserves
   D   It allows each country to adopt an independent monetary policy

Questions: The open economy

7 Which *one* of the following is *not* an economic advantage of international trade?

    A   It encourages international specialisation.
    B   Consumer choice is widened.
    C   It enables industries to secure economies of large-scale production.
    D   Trade surpluses can be used to finance the budget deficit.

8 Which of the following policies for correcting a balance of payments deficit is an expenditure-reducing policy?

    A   Cutting the level of public expenditure
    B   Devaluation of the currency
    C   The imposition of an import tax
    D   The use of import quotas

9 A multi-national company is best described as one which:

    A   Engages extensively in international trade
    B   Sells its output in more than one country
    C   Produces goods or services in more than one country
    D   Is owned by shareholders in more than one country

10 Which of the following is most likely to cause a country's balance of payments to move towards a deficit?

    A   A devaluation of that country's currency
    B   An expansionary fiscal policy
    C   A contractionary fiscal policy
    D   A rise in the rate of domestic saving

11 Which *one* of the following is a characteristic of floating (flexible) exchange rates?

    A   They provide automatic correction for balance of payments deficits and surpluses
    B   They reduce uncertainty for businesses
    C   Transactions costs involved in exchanging currencies are eliminated
    D   They limit the ability of governments to adopt expansionary policies

12 The group of countries that use the euro as their currency is most accurately referred to as:

    A   The European Economic Area (EEA)
    B   The European Union (EU)
    C   The Euro zone
    D   The European Free Trade Association (EFTA)

13 A favourable movement in the terms of trade for a country means that:

    A   The balance of trade has improved
    B   The volume of exports has risen relative to the volume of imports
    C   The prices of exports have risen relative to the prices of imports
    D   The revenue from exports has risen relative to the revenue from imports

14 Which one of the following *cannot* be used to finance a deficit on the current account of a country's balance of payments?

    A   Running down foreign exchange reserves
    B   Increased taxation
    C   Borrowing from foreign central banks
    D   Attracting inflows of short-term capital

Questions: The open economy

15 The imposition of which *one* of the following would *not* act as a barrier to international trade?

    A   A value added tax
    B   Tariffs
    C   Import quotas
    D   Exchange controls

16 Globalisation of capital markets is due to:

    A   International trade in commodities
    B   International trade in microchips
    C   Increasing numbers of expatriate managers
    D   Increasing financial deregulation

17 All of the following are problems of managing international businesses *except* which *one*?

    A   The J-curve effect
    B   Management style
    C   Measuring performance
    D   Staffing

18 A currency devaluation is likely to produce a J-curve effect if:

    A   The terms of trade worsen
    B   Supply and demand are elastic
    C   The terms of trade improve
    D   Supply and demand are inelastic

19 Which of the following is likely to be associated with an improvement in a country's terms of trade?

    A   Increasing levels of imports
    B   Investment producing more sophisticated products
    C   Increasing levels of exports
    D   Investment in cheaper overseas production facilities

20 Assume that two small countries, X and Y, produce two commodities P and Q, and that there are no transport costs. One unit of resource in Country X produces 4 units of P or 8 units of Q. One unit of resource in Country Y produces 1 unit of P or 3 units of Q.

Which *one* of the following statements is *true*?

    A   Country X has an absolute advantage over Country Y in producing P and Q, and so will not trade.
    B   Country X does not have an absolute advantage over Country Y in producing P and Q.
    C   Country Y has a comparative advantage over Country X in producing Q.
    D   Country X has a comparative advantage over Country Y in producing both P and Q.

18 MULTIPLE CHOICE QUESTIONS

1   The table below shows the production capability on one unit of resource in each of two countries, in terms of producing cars and rice.

	Cars		Rice
Bandia	3	or	45 tonnes
Sparta	10	or	60 tonnes

Assume that there are no transport costs, and that opportunity costs are constant for all levels of output. The law of comparative advantage would predict that:

A   Bandia will export rice and Sparta will export cars
B   Sparta will export rice and Bandia will export cars
C   Sparta will export both rice and cars
D   Sparta will export cars and there will be no trade in rice between the countries

2   From a given base year, a country's export prices rise by 8% and import prices rise by 20%. During this period, the terms of trade will have:

A   Risen from 100 to 111.1
B   Risen from 100 to 112
C   Fallen from 100 to 90
D   Fallen from 100 to 88

3   Which of the following items would *not* be included in the UK Balance of Payments statistics?

A   The terms of trade
B   The takeover of a UK company by a Swiss company
C   Investments overseas by private individuals
D   UK government borrowing from International Monetary Fund

4   Which of the following financial transactions will have an adverse effect on the UK's balance of payments, at least in the short run?

1   Increased tourism abroad by UK residents
2   Increased private export of investment capital abroad
3   The payment of cash grant to a developing country by the UK government

A   Item 1 only
B   Items 1 and 2 only
C   Items and 1 and 3 only
D   Items 2 and 3 only

5   If the level of real incomes of the population in the UK were to rise, the UK's balance of payments position would worsen because:

A   The UK's terms of trade would worsen
B   Export prices would rise
C   Import volumes would rise
D   Sterling would appreciate in value

Questions: The open economy

6 The government of a certain country embarks on a policy of reflating the economy. At the same time, it uses its control over interest rates to maintain the stability of the exchange rate for the country's currency. For which of the following reasons might the country's balance of payments go into deficit in the short term?

1 Manufacturers divert goods that would otherwise be exported into domestic markets

2 Foreign investors, attracted by the economic reflation, invest money in the country

3 Economic expansion raises aggregate demand in the economy, so that demand for imports rises

A Reasons 1 and 2 only
B Reasons 1 and 3 only
C Reasons 2 and 3 only
D Reasons 3 only

7 According to the law of comparative advantage, the consequences of protectionism in international trade are that protectionist measures will prevent:

A Each country of the world from maximising its economic wealth

B Each country of the world from maximising the value of its exports

C The countries of the world from maximising their total output with their economic resources

D Each country of the world from achieving equilibrium in its balance of payments

8 In two countries, Lornga and Ziortia, the production of wheat and beef from a given input of factors is as follows.

Lornga: 18 units of wheat or 6 units of beef
Ziortia: 9 units of wheat or 3 units of beef

From this data, it can be deduced that:

A Both countries can benefit from international trade in wheat and beef, because of comparative advantage

B Ziortia cannot benefit from trade in wheat or beef with Lornga, because Ziortia is less efficient in producing both

C Lornga cannot benefit from trade in wheat with Ziortia, because Ziortia's unit costs for wheat will be higher

D Neither country can benefit from trade because their opportunity cost are the same

9 Which of the following items would be in the UK balance of trade statistics?

1 Tourist spending in the UK
2 Accountancy services performed by firms of UK auditors in Germany
3 Timber imported from Scandinavia and re-exported to Spain

A Items 1 and 2 only
B Items 1 and 3 only
C Items 2 and 3 only
D Item 3 only

10 A country's electronics industry, which is its major export industry, switches from the production of mass low-cost, low-profit margin microchips to the production of more high-powered, high-cost, high-profit margin custom-built microchips. The consequence of this switch in production for the country will be:

   A   An improvement in the balance of trade
   B   A deterioration in the balance of trade
   C   An improvement in the terms of trade
   D   A worsening of the terms of trade

11 The UK balance of payments (on current account) will be worsened by all of the following *except* which *one*?

   A   A reduction in spending by overseas tourists in the UK
   B   A reduction in the overseas earnings of UK banks
   C   A reduction in investment in the UK by foreign firms
   D   An increase in the amount of dividends paid by UK subsidiaries of foreign multinational companies

12 Inflation in a country's economy has led to a deterioration in the balance of payments. Which of the following reasons might explain this?

   1   The terms of trade have worsened due to the higher export prices.
   2   Higher domestic prices have made imported goods more attractive.
   3   Excess demand in domestic markets has reduced the volume of goods available for export.

   A   Reasons 1 and 2 only
   B   Reasons 1 and 3 only
   C   Reason 2 only
   D   Reasons 2 and 3 only

13 Reserve currencies are:

   A   Currencies held by governments as part of their gold and foreign currency reserves
   B   Currencies used in some countries as an alternative to their own domestic currency
   C   Money deposited by commercial banks with their central bank, as a means of money supply control
   D   Special drawing rights (SDR) of the International Monetary Fund

14 Devaluation of the currency will:

   A   Improve the terms of trade and *not* increase the cost of living.
   B   Improve the terms of trade but increase the cost of living.
   C   Worsen the terms of trade but *not* increase the cost of living.
   D   Worsen the terms of trade and increase the cost of living.

15 A country's terms of trade improve. Which of the following implications will *necessarily* apply?

   1   The balance of payments on current account will now improve.
   2   The exchange rate will now appreciate in value.
   3   Export prices will already have risen.

   A   Implications 1 and 2 only
   B   Implications 1 and 3 only
   C   Implications 2 and 3 only
   D   None of them necessarily applies

Questions: The open economy

16 If there were an excessive outflow of sterling from the UK, which of the following would you expect to happen?

   A The UK's terms of trade would improve.
   B There would be a revaluation of sterling.
   C Interest rates would fall.
   D There would be a fall in the exchange value of sterling.

17 Suppose that demand for imports in the UK is inelastic. If sterling were to depreciate in value against other countries, which of the following would happen?

	Imports would become	Total spending by the UK on imports
A	Cheaper in sterling	Would rise
B	Cheaper in sterling	Would fall
C	More expensive £ sterling	Would rise
D	More expensive £ sterling	Would fall

18 A country has a balance of trade equal to zero and high imports and exports relative to the size of its National Income. There is then a depreciation of its currency. What will be the consequence or consequences of this depreciation of the currency?

   1 It will improve the terms of trade.
   2 It will improve the balance of trade if the demand for both exports and imports is inelastic.
   3 It might lead to cost-push inflation.

   A Consequences 1 and 2 only
   B Consequences 1 and 3 only
   C Consequences 2 and 3 only
   D Consequence 3 only

19 Gerdaland is a country for which the demand for imports is price inelastic, and the demand for its exports is price elastic. If Gerdaland's domestic currency appreciates in value, which of the following will happen?

   A Exports will increase in value and imports will fall in value.
   B Exports will increase in value and imports will increase in value.
   C Exports will fall in value and imports will fall in value.
   D Exports will fall in value and imports will increase in value.

20 Demand for imports in a country is inelastic and demand for the country's exports is also inelastic in response to price changes. The country's government raises interest rates substantially, and interest rates in other countries remain unchanged. The consequences of the higher interest rates should be:

   A Higher total imports; higher total exports
   B Lower total imports; higher total exports
   C Higher total imports; lower total exports
   D Lower total imports; lower total exports

19 MULTIPLE CHOICE QUESTIONS

1. The following data relates to import prices and export prices of a country over a 3-year period.

    Base year 19X1 = 100

	Unit value of imports	Unit value of exports
19X1	100	100
19X2	112	106
19X3	116	114

    Between 19X2 and 19X3, the country's terms of trade:

    A   Worsened by about 3.7%
    B   Worsened by about 1.7%
    C   Improved by about 1.8%
    D   Improved by about 3.8%

    Data for questions 2 and 3

	19X7 £'000 million	19X8 £'000 million
Visible balance	+6	+18
Invisible balance	+2	+7
Investment abroad	31	27
Investment in the country from abroad	15	12
Lending by domestic banks etc abroad	44	30
Borrowing by residents etc from abroad	49	25
Official reserves (additions to: –, drawings on: +)	–3	–2
Balancing item	+6	–3

2. From the data above, all of the following deductions can be made *except*:

    A   The value of unrecorded items was less in 19X8 than in 19X7
    B   Exports were higher in 19X8 than 19X7
    C   The current balance was more favourable in 19X8 than in 19X7
    D   Official Reserves were higher at the end of 19X8 than at the end of 19X7

3. In 19X8, the current balance was, in £'000 millions:

    A   18
    B   20
    C   22
    D   25

4. In 19X8, transactions in external assets totalled, in £'000 millions:

    A   42
    B   44
    C   57
    D   59

5. In 19X8, transactions in external liabilities totalled, in £'000 millions:

    A   37
    B   39
    C   52
    D   57

Questions: The open economy

6 Suppose that the exchange rate for the euro against the US dollar is 1.1 euros = $1, and the sterling-US dollar exchange rate is $1.50 = £1. If the US dollar depreciates in value against the euro but the sterling-US dollar rate remains stable then, other things being equal:

    A   UK goods will become more expensive in the euro zone but will not change price in the USA

    B   UK and US goods will both become cheaper in the euro zone

    C   US goods will become cheaper in both the UK and the euro zone

    D   US goods will become cheaper in the euro zone and more expensive in the UK

7 Which of the following is a benefit of adopting a single currency within a trading bloc of countries?

    A   Applying a single interest rate to diverse economies
    B   Reduced cost of printing bank notes
    C   More stable exchange rates with the rest of the world
    D   Reduced costs of intra-bloc trade

8 Which *one* of the following will appear in the *current account* of the balance of payments?

    A   Investment income
    B   Portfolio investment
    C   Money brought in by immigrants
    D   Acquisition of financial assets

9 If the exchange rate for a country's currency fell, the result would be that import prices:

    A   Measured in foreign currency would rise
    B   Measured in domestic currency would rise
    C   Measured in foreign currency would fall
    D   Measured in domestic currency would fall

10 Which *one* of the following factors does *not* directly influence a country's exchange rate?

    A   Its level of interest rates
    B   Speculation about its future exchange rate
    C   Its overseas trade
    D   The budget deficit

11 All of the following are characteristic of the process of globalisation *except* which *one*?

    A   An increase in international specialisation
    B   Reduced patent protection for intellectual property
    C   Higher levels of international trade
    D   Increased foreign competition in domestic markets

12 What is the main point of distinction between a free trade area and a customs union?

    A   Free movement of goods and services
    B   Free markets in the factors of production
    C   Common external tariffs
    D   Harmonisation of government excise policy

13 All of the following would normally lead to a rise in the exchange rate for a country's currency, *except* which *one*?

    A   An increase in the country's exports
    B   An increased inflow of foreign direct investment into the country
    C   A rise in interest rates in the country
    D   An increase in the export of capital from the country

Questions: The open economy

14 All of the following are benefits for a business from a depreciation (reduction) in the rate of exchange for the country's currency *except* which *one*?

    A   The business could charge lower prices for its exports.
    B   Imported raw materials used by the business would be cheaper.
    C   The business could raise profit margins on exports without losing sales.
    D   In its home market, the business would face reduced competition from imports.

15 To maximise its gains from trade, a country should:

    A   Try to maximise net exports
    B   Export products in which it has an absolute advantage
    C   Protect domestic producers from competition from cheap imports
    D   Export products in which it has a comparative advantage

16 Multinational companies locate production in more than one country for all of the following reasons *except* which *one*?

    A   The existence of trade barriers
    B   High transport costs
    C   Capital is internationally immobile
    D   To increase market share

17 All of the following are the likely consequences of increased international mobility of factors of production *except* which *one*?

    A   Narrower interest rate differentials between countries
    B   Increased foreign exchange transactions
    C   Increasing differences in average wages between countries
    D   Increased flows of profits, dividends and factor earnings on balance of payments current accounts

18 The terms of trade are defined as:

    A   The ratio of export prices to import prices
    B   The total value of exports minus the total value of imports
    C   The change in volume of exports compared to changes in the volume of imports
    D   The commercial conditions under which international trade takes place

19 The balance of payments accounts are defined as:

    A   The difference between the government's receipts and its expenditure over the period of a year
    B   The difference between the exports of goods and services and imports of goods and services over the period of a year
    C   The surplus or deficit on a country's international trade over a given period
    D   A statement of the economic transactions between residents of a country and the rest of the world over a given period

20 All of the following statements are true *except* which *one*?

    A   Import quotas tend to reduce prices
    B   Trade protection tends to reduce consumer choice
    C   Trade protection tends to reduce exports
    D   Tariffs tend to reduce competition

Questions: The open economy

20 OBJECTIVE TEST QUESTIONS

1. A country has a comparative advantage over another country when it can produce more of a good from a given amount of resources.
   - [ ] True
   - [ ] False

2. Country X and Country Y each produce both guns and butter. Using the same total amount of resources to produce either guns or butter, the two countries can achieve the output shown below.

	Guns	Butter (tons)
Country X	20	200
Country Y	10	150

   According to the law of comparative advantage (comparative costs), should Country Y import guns or butter from Country X?
   - [ ] Guns
   - [ ] Butter

3. Dumping is a form of trade protection in which onerous administrative requirements are imposed in order to hamper importers.
   - [ ] True
   - [ ] False

4. A regional trading bloc must use a single currency for its transactions.
   - [ ] True
   - [ ] False

5. Fill in the missing word in the sentence below.

   If it wishes to control a rising exchange rate, the central bank will ▓▓▓▓▓▓▓▓▓▓ the supply of its currency to the market.

6. A fixed exchange rate is not normally compatible in the long term with different inflation rates in the countries concerned.
   - [ ] True
   - [ ] False

7. State whether a marked deterioration in the UK's balance of trade is likely to lead to an increase or a decrease in the value of sterling.
   - [ ] Increase
   - [ ] Decrease

8. Which of the following are characteristics of a common market?
   - A Harmonisation of levels of direct taxation
   - B Common external tariffs
   - C Free trade among members
   - D Free movement of factors of production between member countries

Questions: The open economy

9   Strike out the incorrect **bold** word in the sentence below.

    A rise in interest rates will enlarge a **surplus/deficit** on the balance of trade.

10 Name the axes of the J curve shown below.

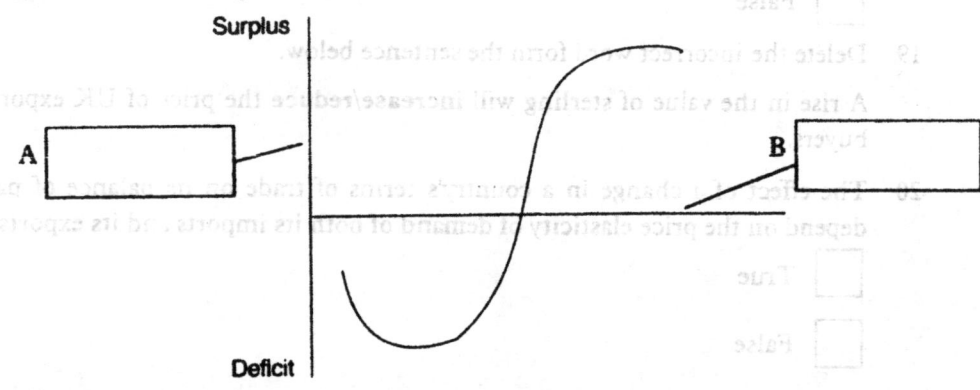

    A: _____   B: _____

11 On the currency markets, a spot rate is valid for immediate delivery only.

    ☐ True
    ☐ False

12 The J curve effect prevents devaluation from having a long term effect on a country's balance of trade.

    ☐ True
    ☐ False

13 State whether a firm decision for the UK to join the European single currency (the euro) is likely to be associated with an increase or a decrease in the value of sterling.

    ☐ Increase
    ☐ Decrease

14 A country's balance of trade is determined by the prices of its imports and exports.

    ☐ True
    ☐ False

15 Insert the missing word in the sentence below.

    A country's terms of trade will worsen if its ▮▮▮▮▮▮▮▮▮ rate falls.

16 Bonjovia's terms of trade have declined in 2003 to 80% of their 2002 value.

    Index numbers for import and export prices for the two years are given below.

    What is the missing index number?

	Exports	Imports
2002	150	???
2003	144	216

17 Insert the missing word in the sentence below.

    The great disadvantage of the euro currency system is that member countries lose all control over ▮▮▮▮▮▮▮▮▮ policy.

69

Questions: The open economy

18 Imports are never a source of demand pull inflation.

☐ True

☐ False

19 Delete the incorrect word form the sentence below.

A rise in the value of sterling will **increase/reduce** the price of UK exports to foreign buyers.

20 The effect of a change in a country's terms of trade on its balance of payments will depend on the price elasticity of demand of both its imports and its exports.

☐ True

☐ False

Questions 21 and 22 cover the complete syllabus for Paper 3a.

21 MULTIPLE CHOICE QUESTIONS

1 Governments could raise labour productivity by all of the following *except* which *one*?

    A   Providing tax relief for research and development expenditure by companies
    B   Increasing expenditure on education and training
    C   Reducing discrimination in employment practices
    D   Reducing social security payments

2 Diseconomies of scale occur in a business when:

    A   Minimum efficient scale is reached
    B   Short-run variable costs begin to rise
    C   X-inefficiency begins
    D   Long-run average costs begin to rise

3 If the demand for a good increases, which *one* of the following will occur?

    A   Price rises and the quantity sold falls.
    B   Price falls and the quantity sold rises.
    C   Price and quantity sold both rise.
    D   Price and quantity sold both fall.

4 The economic problem of what to produce is concerned with:

    A   Which goods and services and how much of each are to be produced
    B   Which goods will meet individual and social needs
    C   Which goods will maximise the rate of growth of welfare over time
    D   Which combination of resources should be used in production

5 Which *one* of the following will produce the largest fluctuations in a market price?

    A   Large shifts in supply with price elastic demand
    B   Large shifts in supply with price inelastic demand
    C   Large shifts in supply with perfectly price elastic demand
    D   Small shifts in supply with price inelastic demand

6 Which *one* of the following is *not* a potential source of market failure?

    A   External costs
    B   External benefits
    C   An unequal income distribution
    D   The existence of monopolies

7 The kinked demand curve model of oligopoly is designed to explain:

    A   Price leadership
    B   Price rigidity
    C   Collusion between producers
    D   Price competition

8 Under monopolistic competition, excess profits are eliminated in the long run because of:

    A   The lack of barriers to entry
    B   The effects of product differentiation
    C   The existence of excess capacity
    D   The downward sloping demand curve for the product

71

Questions: Complete syllabus

9 The economic welfare case for governments increasing taxes on petrol to raise its real price is that:

    A   Oil is a scarce resource
    B   It would reduce the imports of oil
    C   There is a large demand for petrol
    D   Petrol consumption involves external social costs

10 All of the following would lead to an upward shift in a firm's demand curve for labour *except* which *one*?

    A   An increase in the demand for the firm's product
    B   An increase in the productivity of labour
    C   A fall in the price of labour
    D   A rise in the price of substitute factors of production

11 Gross national product will be higher than gross domestic product if:

    A   Exports of goods and services exceed imports of goods and services
    B   There is a net inflow of factor payments on the current account of the balance of payments
    C   There is a net inflow on the capital account of the balance of payments
    D   Government taxation exceeds government expenditure

12 In the circular flow model of the economy, the level of national income will always reach an equilibrium because:

    A   Injections and withdrawals are always equal
    B   Withdrawals are a function of the level of income
    C   Governments will change taxes and expenditure to ensure equilibrium
    D   Expenditure equals income

13 All of the following are disadvantages of inflation *except* which *one*?

    A   It redistributes wealth from debtors to creditors
    B   It reduces international competitiveness
    C   Market price signals are distorted
    D   Fixed income earners experience a fall in real income

14 Cyclical unemployment is unemployment:

    A   That occurs because of the seasonal nature of some industries
    B   Resulting from the long-term decline of an industry
    C   That occurs at particular times of the year
    D   That occurs during recessions

15 What is linked to the exchange rate over the long run, according to purchasing power parity theory?

    A   Levels of economic welfare
    B   Levels of national income
    C   Rates of inflation
    D   Interest rates

16 The crowding out effect occurs when a:

    A   Rise in interest rates reduces private investment
    B   Rise in interest rates reduces the demand for money
    C   Fall in interest rates discourages saving
    D   Rise in interest rates raises mortgage rates

Questions: Complete syllabus

17 An expansionary fiscal policy would be most likely to reduce unemployment if the country had:

    A   A high marginal propensity to import
    B   A low marginal propensity to save
    C   A high marginal tax rate
    D   A low marginal propensity to consume

18 The effect on a business of contractionary fiscal policy will be greatest when the business:

    A   Has a high gearing ratio
    B   Produces a good with a high income elasticity of demand
    C   Produces non-durable goods
    D   Exports a high proportion of its output

19 The real rate of interest is defined as the:

    A   Rate of interest banks actually charge their customers
    B   Annualised percentage rate of interest
    C   Yield on undated fixed interest government securities
    D   Difference between the money rate of interest and the inflation rate

20 If a country can produce all goods more efficiently than its trading partner, it should export:

    A   No goods
    B   Only those goods in which it has an absolute advantage
    C   Only those goods in which its efficiency advantage is greatest
    D   All goods

22 MULTIPLE CHOICE QUESTIONS

1 All of the following are reasons for trans-national companies locating production of a good in more than one country *except* which *one*?

    A   The existence of trade barriers
    B   Significant transport costs
    C   Economise of scale in production
    D   Differences in demand conditions between countries

2 An increase in the international mobility of factors of production leads to:

    A   An increase in international trade
    B   Increased unemployment in low wage economies
    C   Increasing differences in wage rates between countries
    D   Decreasing differences in factor prices between countries

3 All of the following are characteristics of the process of globalisation *except* which *one*?

    A   Increased international specialisation
    B   Greater integration of production in manufacturing
    C   Higher levels of international trade
    D   Movement of manufacturing industries to low labour cost locations

4 All of the following are characteristics of a common market *except* which *one*?

    A   Free trade in goods and services among member states
    B   Common levels of direct taxation
    C   Free movement of factors of production between member states
    D   A common external tariff

5 Which *one* of the following would be likely to result in a rise in the value of UK sterling against the euro?

    A   A rise in interest rates in the UK
    B   The UK central bank buying euros in exchange for sterling
    C   A rise in interest rates in the euro zone
    D   Increased capital flows form the UK to the euro zone

6 Which *one* of the following would lead *directly* to an outward shift in a country's production possibility frontier?

    A   A rise in the population of working age
    B   A fall in unemployment
    C   An increase in outward migration
    D   A rise in the school leaving age

7 The cost of one good or service measured in terms of what must be sacrificed to obtain it is called:

    A   Real cost
    B   Potential cost
    C   Opportunity cost
    D   Social cost

8 All of the following are supply side policies which would promote economic growth *except* which *one*?

    A   Increased expenditure on education and training
    B   A reduction in marginal rates of taxation
    C   Deregulation of industry and finance
    D   Increase social welfare expenditure

Questions: Complete syllabus

9 All of the following are essential features of a market economy *except* which *one*?

- A Private ownership of productive resources
- B Allocation of resources by the price mechanism
- C Absence of entry and exit barriers to and from industries
- D Prices determined by market forces

10 The profit-maximising output will always be where:

- A Average cost = Marginal revenue
- B Marginal cost = Marginal revenue
- C Average cost = Average revenue
- D Marginal cost = Average revenue

11 If a business currently sells 10,000 units of its product each month at $10 each unit and the demand for its products has a price elasticity of −2.5, a rise in the price of the produce to $11 will:

- A Raise total revenue by $7,250
- B Reduce total revenue by $17,500
- C Reduce total revenue by $25,000
- D Raise total revenue by $37,500

12 In a kinked demand curve model of oligopoly, the kink in the firm's demand curve is due to the firm's belief that competitors will:

- A Set a price at the kink of the demand curve
- B Match all price increases and price reductions
- C Match any price increases, but not any price reductions
- D Match any price reductions, but not any price increases

13 Which one of the following is a natural barrier to the entry of new firms into an industry?

- A Large initial capital costs
- B The issuing of patents
- C A government awarded franchise
- D The licensing of professions

14 A good which is characterised by both rivalry and excludability is called:

- A A public good
- B A private good
- C A government good
- D An external good

15 The burden of an indirect tax on a good will fall more heavily on the producer when:

- A Demand for the good is price elastic
- B Demand for the good is price inelastic
- C Demand for the good has unit elasticity
- D Supply of the good is price elastic

16 In practice, a monopoly may have its market power limited by all of the following *except* which *one*?

- A Countervailing power from its customers
- B The market may be contestable
- C There may be close substitutes for the good
- D The firm's long-run average cost curve may be falling

75

Questions: Complete syllabus

17 All of the following are examples of where externalities are likely to occur *except* which *one*?

    A   A business providing training scheme for its employees
    B   Government expenditure on vaccination programmes for infectious diseases
    C   Attending a concert given by a government-funded orchestra
    D   Private motorists driving cars in city centres

18 Whenever government intervention prevents prices from reaching their equilibrium level, the result will always include all of the following *except* which *one*?

    A   Shortages or surpluses
    B   Demand and supply not equal
    C   Reduced profits for producers
    D   Resources not allocated by price

19 Which *one* of the following would cause the multiplier to fall?

    A   A fall in the level of government expenditure
    B   A rise in the marginal propensity to consume
    C   A rise in business investment
    D   A rise in the marginal propensity to save

20 The linking of net savers with net borrowers is known as:

    A   The savings function
    B   Financial intermediation
    C   Financial regulation
    D   A store of value

Answer

Answers   Notes

1   MULTIPLE CHOICE QUESTIONS

1   B   This is a good definition of opportunity cost.
2   C   This is the signalling function of the price mechanism.
3   C   The money spent could have been used for other things.
4   B   Incomes will be mainly determined by labour market conditions.
5   A   Scarcity of resources available to meet needs is the key feature.
6   D   A mixed economy combines aspects of the market economy and the planned economy.
7   D   Consumer wants are treated as potentially unlimited, but resources are scarce.
8   B   Opportunity cost concerns the next best alternative forgone.
9   C   'Opportunity cost of products' is not relevant.
10 D   Structural unemployment is likely since growth implies the development of new industries and the decline of old ones.
11 D   There is likely to be a stock market in a mixed economy.
12 D   The basic economic problem is one of scarce resources and economics is the study of how those resources are or should be used.
13 A   A planned economy or command economy is one in which economic decisions about resource application are taken by a central body, the 'state'. It is in free market economies and mixed economies that factors B, C and D influence resource allocation.
14 B   In a free market economy, it is the interaction of supply and demand through the price mechanism that determines what should be produced and who should get it.
15 C   The primary sector is usually defined to include agriculture and the extractive industries, the secondary sector to include manufacturing and construction and the tertiary sector to include service industries. Farming and quarrying are in the primary sector and banking in the tertiary sector.
16 B   Unemployment is more likely to be falling than rising, so payments should decline.
17 D   This question calls for a straightforward definition of opportunity cost.
18 D   That which is given up.
19 C   Existing capital would run out sooner and less would be replaced.
20 A   This is merely a use of production.

2   MULTIPLE CHOICE QUESTIONS

1   D   This would encourage consumption rather than investment.
2   B   The compensation is an economic cost for the firm.
3   D   Productivity is primarily about efficiency.
4   B   This may inhibit economic growth as spending will be reduced.
5   B   Much production is likely to be in private ownership.
6   A   Positive economics has been contrasted with 'normative' economics.

79

Notes	Answers		
	7	C	Management is a specialised type of labour. A, B and D are factors of production; the missing factor is **land**.
	8	B	Positive economics is concerned with objective description and explanation of the economic world as it actually exists.
	9	C	This is likely to reduce the size of the working population, which will tend to reduce output. Option A will lead directly to increased output; option B is likely to result in greater individual productivity; and option D is likely to lead to a larger population of working age and thence to increased output.
	10	D	There is no special term for options A and C; option B is the growth rate in money terms, as opposed to real terms.
	11	D	Externalities can be either positive or negative; extraction of natural resources presupposes an ultimate limit to their availability; the requirement for new skills may leave some sections of the population unemployed and even unemployable.
	12	A	Fantasia currently produces 13 guns and 4,000 tons of butter. If production of guns were reduced to 9 and all resources were used effectively, production of butter would rise to about 6,700 tons, an increase of 2,700 tons. An increase of about 1,500 tons to 5,500 could be expected if production continued at about its current state of efficiency (a move to point E on the diagram below).

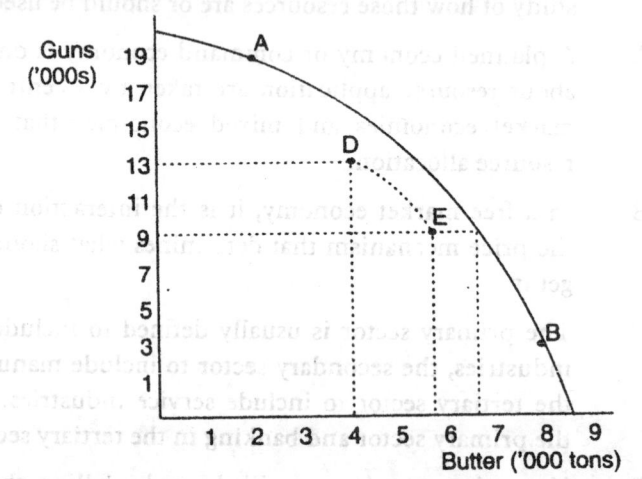

	13	D	The production possibility curve is a theoretical maximum: many factors may prevent an economy from achieving its theoretical maximum output. One of these is unemployment, which is, effectively, a failure to use all the available labour resources. A fall in unemployment will thus push output closer to its potential but will not increase that potential. Changes in prices may take effect through the macroeconomy to affect the level of actual output via complex mechanisms, but they cannot in themselves change the potential level of output.
	14	A	Attempts have been made to abolish money in centrally planned economies but they were not successful: money is required at least at a unit of account. The sad history of central planning is that in a mature economy it is grossly inefficient compared to the invisible hand of the market, and cannot approach the wealth-creating potential of the market-based system.
	15	B	It is probably impossible to have a mixed economy without a democracy and *vice versa*, but democracy is a political term while mixed economy is an economic one. A market economy (option C), strictly speaking, has no place for government intervention, as for instance in the provision of welfare. A common market (option D) is an international free trade area with a common external tariff and free movement within it of the factors of production.

Answers   Notes

16 C Options A, B and D are red herrings.
17 D All of the changes should shift the frontier outwards.
18 A Expectation of future growth will contribute to business confidence and thus to willingness to invest.
19 C Option A is incorrect because no task has been divided up. Option B *may* occur if the displaced crew members are unable to find other employment but is not an inevitable consequence. Option C is correct because fewer labour hours are now required for a given output.
20 B This is not an easy question to answer. However, of the options, C is definitely wrong: the labour markets of European countries are more highly regulated than that of the USA. Population size differences should not really affect growth potential, though a very small country might find it difficult to support an advanced technological base. Option B, advanced technology, is widely recognised as a major contributor to the USA's generally high level of growth.

3 MULTIPLE CHOICE QUESTIONS

1 C The other options relate to movements *along* the supply curve.
2 C Supply will extend and demand will contract.
3 A The change in revenue is the same as the fall in price. Therefore there is no change in volume.
4 D A rise in the exchange rate is effectively a reduction in price.
5 A This is about substituting other factors for labour because its price has gone up. Options B and C encourage the substitution and option D makes it easy. Only option A makes substitution unlikely.
6 B This is a classic example of the operation of diminishing returns.
7 D Technical improvements could apply at any scale of operations.
8 B Perfect competition requires a homogeneous product. Product differentiation is an important aspect of monopolistic competition.
9 D Monopolistic competition involves a number of competing producers. A market with one dominant producer is somewhere between oligopoly and monopoly.
10 B Generally, if incomes fall, demand will fall.
11 A There is no differentiation under perfect competition.
12 C Demand will transfer to the substitute.
13 A This is a transfer payment
14 B This is an input into the picture framing industry.
15 D This may make carpet less desirable, but it is not a substitute for it. Some kind of finish to the floor will still be required.
16 C An increase in demand for carpets will lead to an increase in demand for their complements.
17 B This is a supply-side factor.
18 C Any unilateral price change brings a disadvantage to the supplier concerned.
19 D Examples would include some utilities, which usually involve an extensive capital infrastructure.

81

Notes	Answers		
	20	C	They also equal both marginal revenue and average revenue.

4   MULTIPLE CHOICE QUESTIONS

1	B	Any business may require both capital and skilled labour. Diseconomies of scale will tend to limit growth, not entry.
2	D	Monopolies tend to produce at a level below that which offers the lowest average cost.
3	C	The monopolist faces market demand since there are no other producers.
4	C	This is related to the trade cycle.
5	D	This involves regulations favouring producers rather than consumers.
6	C	Apply the points of definition of a public good if you are unsure about this.
7	B	The size of the elasticity is then greater than 1.
8	D	Fixed costs are fixed and both marginal and average variable cost may fall before diminishing returns occur.
9	D	Do not confuse the long and short run effects: these are diseconomies of scale and diminishing returns respectively.
10	A	The other choices are external economies of scale: bulk buying is internal.
11	A	The other options are not always true.
12	C	Homogeneity means the producers are in competition with one another.
13	A	A classic example of a public good.
14	C	Do not confuse with D, which is simply 'rent'.
15	B	The elasticity of supply of the final product will not be an influencing factor.
16	A	A point of definition.
17	C	B is the income effect.
18	B	Geographic mobility of labour implies something other than commuting!
19	B	A reduction in income tax will increase real household income, and so demand for normal products will shift to the right – quantity demanded will be greater at any given price. Items A and D will cause a leftward shift in the demand curve. Item C would cause a movement to the right along the demand curve.
20	D	Coffee and tea are substitute products. Thus, a fall in the price of coffee will result in higher demand for coffee and lower demand for its substitute product, tea. The price of tea might therefore fall. Demand for drinking cups is probably insufficiently related to the consumption of coffee to make them a complementary product to coffee. Even so, lower coffee prices would be likely to raise the demand for drinking cups rather than reduce it.

5   MULTIPLE CHOICE QUESTIONS

1	D	The term 'inferior good' is a technical term in economics. An example of such a good might be small 'starter' homes.
2	D	It is assumed that cut flowers and flower vases are complementary goods. The rise in price of cut flowers will have an adverse effect on demand for flower vases, and the demand curve for flower vases will shift to the left. Given no change in supply conditions for vases, the new equilibrium price for vases will be lower.

Answers Notes

3 A **Statement 1** is incorrect. When demand is price elastic, a fall in price will *increase* total spending on the good. **Statement 2** is incorrect, because when household income rises, demand for an inferior good will fall: income elasticity of demand will be negative, not zero. **Statement 3** is incorrect. If goods A and B are complements, a rise in the price of B will cause a fall in the demand for A, and so cross elasticity of demand is negative.

4 A **Statement A** is correct: demand will tend to be elastic when the product has a large number of close substitutes. The rate of consumption and the variety of uses for a product could be irrelevant to **elasticity**. However, a high *rate* of demand/consumption might suggest consumer goods, which tend to have elastic demand. **Statement C** is incorrect. If a product is bought by people on subsistence incomes, a rise in its price is unlikely to result in higher total spending on the product (ie demand will *not* be inelastic) and if demand switches to cheaper substitutes, which is likely, demand for the product will be price elastic. Product with a wide range of uses tend to have a variety of substitutes (eg butter) and so demand is quite likely to be elastic.

5 A Widgets and splodgets are complements. when the price of splodgets goes up by 10%, demand for widgets will go **down** by (× 0.6) 6% at that price. The demand curve for widgets has shifted to the left, and a new equilibrium price and output quantity will be established, at a lower output and price. However, since we do not know what the supply curve for widgets is, we cannot say what the new equilibrium price will be.

6 B A rise in the price of a good bought by people on subsistence incomes is likely to make them switch their buying to other (substitute) products, and so demand for the good will tend to be elastic. A fall in the price of the product will have a reverse effect, making consumers demand significantly more of the product since it is now relatively cheaper than before, compared to the price of substitutes.

7 D

	Cost of 100 units £	Cost of 101 units £
Total variable cost	200	202
Total fixed cost	100	100
Total cost	300	302
Average cost	£3.00	£2.99

The marginal cost is £2, which is the increase in the total variable cost and also the increase in the total cost, since fixed costs are the same at both volumes of output.

8 C Proposition 3 is false: it is **average** fixed costs per unit (AFC) that fall as output increases. Marginal fixed cots = 0. Since AFC falls, any fall in average variable cost (AVC) must mean a falling average total cost (ATC) since AVC + AFC = ATC. Proposition 2 must therefore be false.

9 A In conditions of perfect competition, the firm can sell whatever output it produces at the market price. The demand curve is the marginal revenue curve, as well as the average revenue curve (ie price curve).

10 C Predatory pricing is the name sometimes given to the temporary lowering of prices by a monopolist, to deter other firms which might be considering entry into the market, so Statement C is incorrect.

Notes   Answers

Statement A is correct. By having over-capacity a monopolist can deter would-be rivals from entering the market. This is because it would be able to threaten an increase in output, lower production costs and so lower and more competitive prices.

Statement B is correct. When economies of scale are achievable at high volumes of output, a single firm should be able to monopolise the market by producing most of the market output at a cost (and price) that rivals cannot match.

Statement D is correct. When barriers to **exit** from a market are low, because a firm will suffer **few** or no (sunk) cost if it decides to leave the market, the market will become more contestable.

11 B   Statement A is correct because it is an example of the same product being sold at two or more different prices, according to the time of day. Statement D is true: the same good or service may be sold at different prices in different geographical areas, to people of different ages (eg half price for children), on the basis of time (eg see Statement A) or because consumers in one market are ignorant of lower prices in another market. Statement C is correct, because price discrimination for a good in two geographical markets can only be sustained if it is too expensive for a customer to buy goods in the low-price market, incur transport costs to ship them to the higher –price market, and sell them at a competitive price in that market. Statement B is incorrect, because production costs should not have any influence on price discrimination, only a firm's output levels.

12 D   A pension relates to former employment. All the other rewards relate to current earnings for factors currently employed.

13 A   This is assumed to be the basic aim.

14 B   This defines the short run.

15 C   'Normal profit' is that earned by companies in conditions of perfect competition and represents compensation for the risks borne by the entrepreneur or provider of capital.

16 B   Sea ferry tickets and hovercraft tickets for Channel crossings are presumable substitute goods. An increase in the price of hovercraft tickets will cause a shift to the right (increase in demand) for sea ferry tickets. Given no change in supply conditions, the consequence will be an increase in the number of sea ferry tickets sold, at a higher price than before.

17 D   All three factors influence elasticity of supply. Supply is usually more elastic in the longer term than the short term, in response to price changes, because in the short term, more resources are 'fixed' and committed to producing the good. The supply curve for a good is the sum of the **marginal cost curves** of all firms in the industry and the slope of the curve – ie elasticity – will therefore be dependent on marginal costs. Supply is also more elastic when producers have more readily-available production opportunities that they can switch their resources to.

18 B

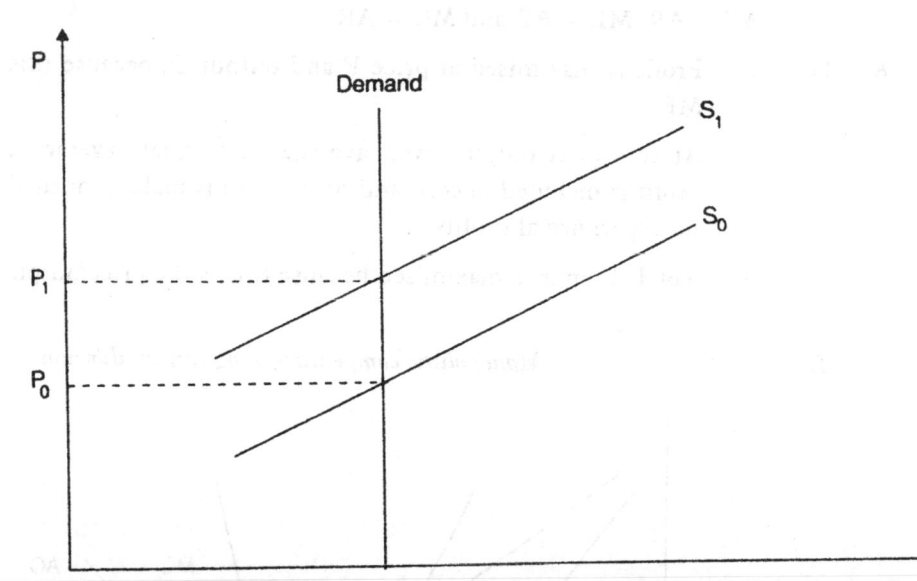

The effect of the increase in tax is to shift the supply curve from S₀ to S₁, the vertical difference between S₀ and S₁ being the amount of the tax. The price change, from P₀ to P₁, is the amount of the tax, which is fully borne by the consumer. Demand volume remains unchanged.

19 B Oddly enough, advertising (a form of non-price competition) is more likely to be successful for products with a low price elasticity of demand – ie for products whose demand is influenced by factors other than price. **Statements A and D** are incorrect because the supply curves of the product will be unaffected. **Statement C** is not necessarily correct because the higher total profits (and revenue) from their higher price will not necessarily cover the costs of the advertising.

20 A

	£
Cost of 31 men per hour (× £5.50)	170.50
Cost of 30 men per hour (× £5)	150.00
Marginal cost	20.50

6 MULTIPLE CHOICE QUESTIONS

1 D When price elasticity of demand is 1, any change in price will result in a change in quantity demanded, so that total revenue remains unchanged. This means that MR must be zero (since any change in output will leave revenue the same) and that total revenue must be at a maximum (since any change in price/output will leave revenue the same). Statement 2 is wrong, since the average revenue (ie price) must change with output for total revenue to remain unchanged.

2 C Normal profit is an element of cost, in the economist's approach.

3 A To the extent that the guard protects society against crime, his costs are a social benefit rather than a social cost. Statements 1 and 2 are correct, however, for the reasons explained in each statement.

4 B Item 2 is an example of an external diseconomy of scale. If an industry grows in size, the competition for resources can push up their cost. For example, skilled labour shortages might occur and push up wage rates. Item 3 is an example of an internal diseconomy of scale. Employees who enjoy working for a smaller firm might become demotivated and less productive as the firm grows into something more bureaucratic and less friendly.

Notes   Answers

5   D   At a profit maximising equilibrium, MR = AR = AC = MC and so MC = MR, AC = AR, MR = AR and MC = AR.

6   D   1   Profit is maximised at price P and output Q, because this is where MC = MR.

2   At this price/output level, average cost equals average revenue. Normal profit is included in cost, and so the firm is making normal profits only, but no supernormal profits.

3   Total revenue is maximised because this is the price/output level where MR = 0.

7   B

Monopolistic competition: long run equilibrium

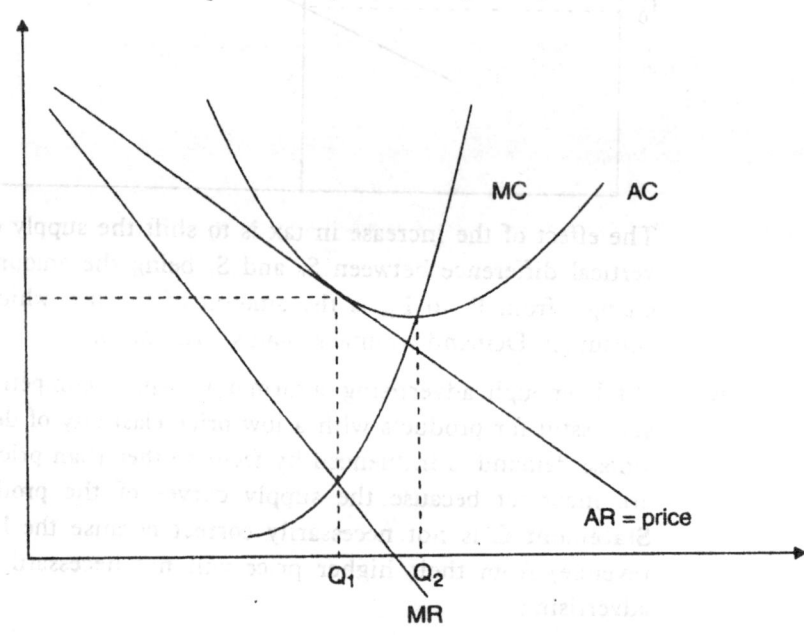

For long run equilibrium in monopolistic competition, MR = MC and AR = AC, but it is **wrong** to say that MR = AC (Statement A) or that AR = MC (Statement D). Since AR = AC, the firm does **not** earn any supernormal profits (Statement C). Statement B is correct because at the profit-maximising output Q_1, average cost is not at a minimum. AC is minimised at output Q_2, which is higher. Since firms could produce more output at a lower AC, we would say that there is excess capacity in the industry.

8   D   First and second class tickets are not an example of price discrimination, because even though they are tickets for the same aeroplane journey, they are different products – eg in terms of service and travel comfort – rather than the same product being sold at two or more different prices. All the other statements are true, with B and C being key conditions for price discrimination to be achievable.

9   C   This question presumes that you know that a perfectly competitive firm can sell all its extra output at the same price as previous output. This means that the extra output will have a higher MRP in a perfectly competitive environment than in the case of Muscles Ltd, which must reduce its prices, and earn progressively less marginal revenue, to sell more.

10 C

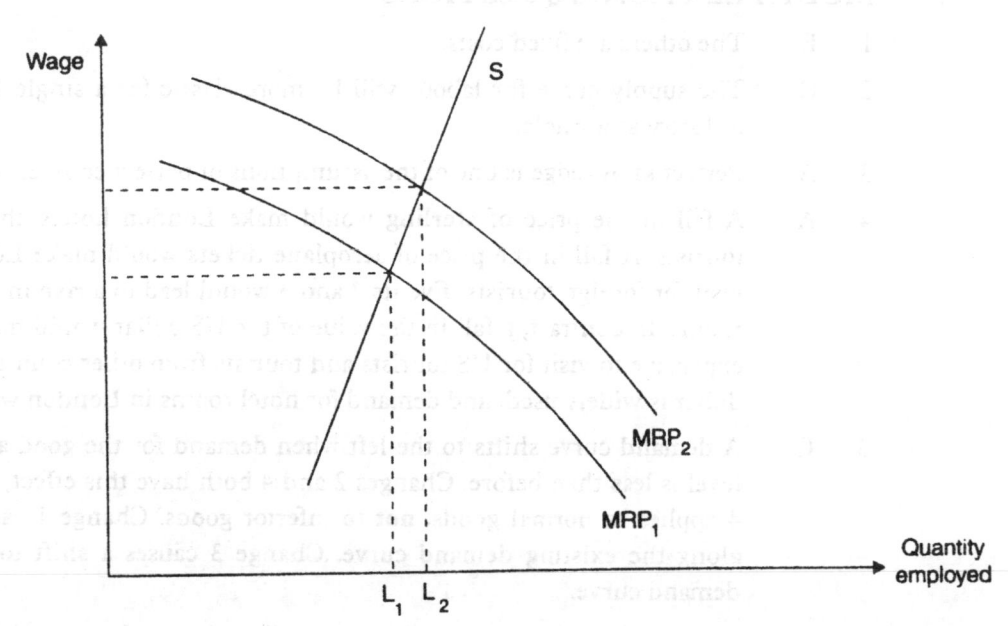

Graph: Wage vs Quantity employed, showing supply curve S, and two MRP curves MRP₁ and MRP₂, with equilibrium points at L₁ and L₂.

The diagram shows that a shift in the MRP of labour due to productivity improvements, from MRP₁ to MRP₂, will result in a relatively small increase in employment numbers from L₁ to L₂ and a relatively large increase in wages from W₁ to W₂.

11 B   Social cost is the sum of the private cost to a firm *plus* the external cost to society as a whole. Here, social cost is the sum of production costs (private costs) plus the cost of pollution (external cost). The firm's private costs might have been increased by the measures to reduce pollution, but the external costs will have fallen, so that total social costs should have fallen too.

12 B   They apply over the long run, when all factors are subject to change.

13 D   The demand for the good will be highly price inelastic.

14 B   Costs are irrelevant. Identical PED means identical response to price changes. D is likely to follow after C.

15 A   Refer to your Study Text if in doubt.

16 D   Since elasticity of demand = 1, the total revenue from selling an extra unit would remain unchanged (the quantity sold would fall) and MR = 0. Since MC = $25, there would be an incremental loss of $25.

17 B   Diminishing returns face **all** firms, small and large, in the short run. Large firms should not expand output in the **short run** to a level where diminishing returns are obtained, if they wish to maximise profits. However, in the **longer run**, they can expand without facing diminishing returns at higher output volumes. Do not confuse diminishing returns with diseconomies of scale, which large firms **might** eventually suffer from if they get bigger.

18 B   The law of variable proportions is another name for the law of diminishing returns, which refers to the short run when at least one factor of production is fixed. Since **all** inputs are increased by 50% we must be looking at the long run average cost curve, and in this example, at decreasing returns to scale, since the percentage increase in inputs exceeds the percentage increase in outputs.

19 B   The market has nothing to do with income.

20 C   This makes entry and exit easy.

Notes   **Answers**

7 MULTIPLE CHOICE QUESTIONS

1 B The others are fixed costs.

2 C The supply curve for labour will be more elastic for a single firm than for the industry as a whole.

3 A Perfect knowledge is one of the assumptions of perfect competition.

4 A A fall in the price of **sterling** would make London hotels cheaper for foreign tourists. A fall in the price of aeroplane tickets would make London cheaper to visit for foreign tourists. Events 2 and 3 would lead to a **rise** in demand for hotel rooms. In contrast, a fall in the value of the US dollar would make the UK more expensive to visit for US tourists and tourists from other countries where the US dollar is widely used, and demand for hotel rooms in London would fall.

5 C A demand curve shifts to the left when demand for the good at any given price level is less than before. Changes 2 and 4 both have this effect, although Change 4 applies to normal goods, **not** to inferior goods. Change 1 causes a movement along the existing demand curve. Change 3 causes a shift to the **right** of the demand curve.

6 B When rent controls are eased, the effect is similar to raising or removing minimum prices in the rented housing market. We should expect higher rents, more supply of housing, and a closing of the gap between demand for rented housing and supply of rented accommodation. Changes 2 and 3 should therefore occur. The reverse of Change 1 should happen, and homelessness should decrease. Given widespread homelessness, it is unlikely that the easing of rent controls will have any effect on demand for owner-occupied dwellings.

7 A This is best illustrated by a diagram.

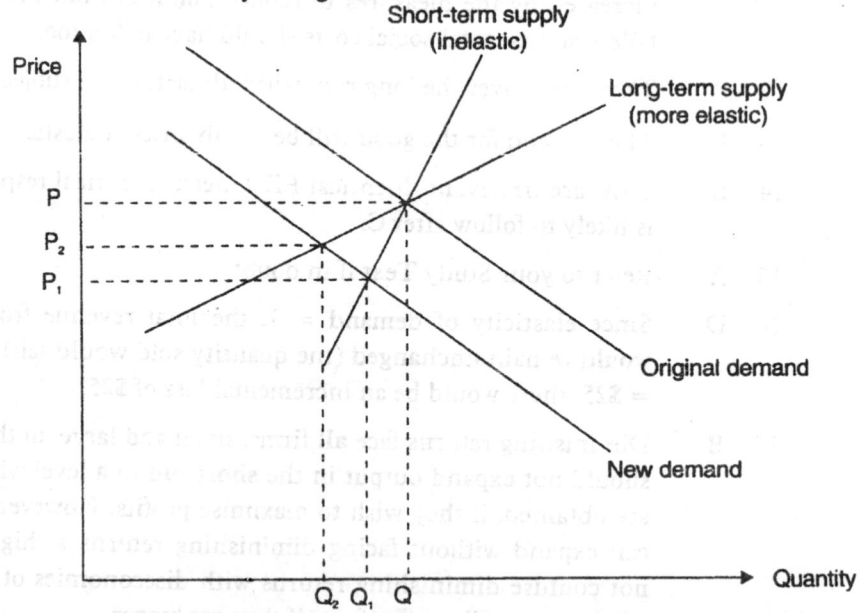

The original equilibrium is price P and output Q. When demand falls, supply will fall in the short run to Q_1 and the price will fall to P_1. In the longer term, supply capacity is reduced, and the supply curve becomes more elastic. The output quantity falls further to Q_2, and price recovers to P_2, which is less than the original equilibrium price P.

8	C	Cross elasticity of demand = $\dfrac{\text{\% change in quantity of good A demanded *}}{\text{\% change in the price of good B}}$

*given no change in the price of A

If Smudge Paints puts its prices up, we should expect customers to switch to buying more from Dogsbrush; hence cross elasticity of demand is positive. Since the products are in direct competition with each other, the cross elasticity of demand should be high.

9	D	This enables them to make super-normal profit.
10	C	The variable cost per unit is sometimes used as another way of explaining marginal cost, but only in the sense that we mean the variable cost of the next unit produced. Since the MC per unit varies with output (according to the law of diminishing returns) the **average** variable cost for all units produced will not be the same as the marginal cost of the next unit. The other statements are correct: Statement A is true because average fixed costs per unit decline continuously as output increases. Statement D is correct because MC includes normal profit as a cost.
11	D	Do not confuse this with economies of scale.
12	C	The company is running the same services as before, and so is not expanding its output and economies of scale are not achieved here. The lower costs per passenger mile will be the result of a reduction in the work force from 8 to just 4.
13	B	If a firm makes 1,000 units of output using 10 units of labour and 10 units of capital, say, it is **technically efficient** if a reduction in the mount of labour or capital will mean that the firm cannot make 1,000 units of output any more. There is no resource wastage. A firm can be technically efficient combining inputs in a number of different ways or mixes to produce a given quantity of output, and so in this example, the firm could produce 1,000 units with a variety of different mixes of labour and capital. If it produces the 1,000 units with the mix that minimises average cost, the firm is **economically efficient**.
14	B	If wages account for a **higher** proportion of total costs, the demand for labour is likely to be **more** elastic, since a rise in labour costs would have a bigger effect on costs of production.

Notes   Answers

15   B

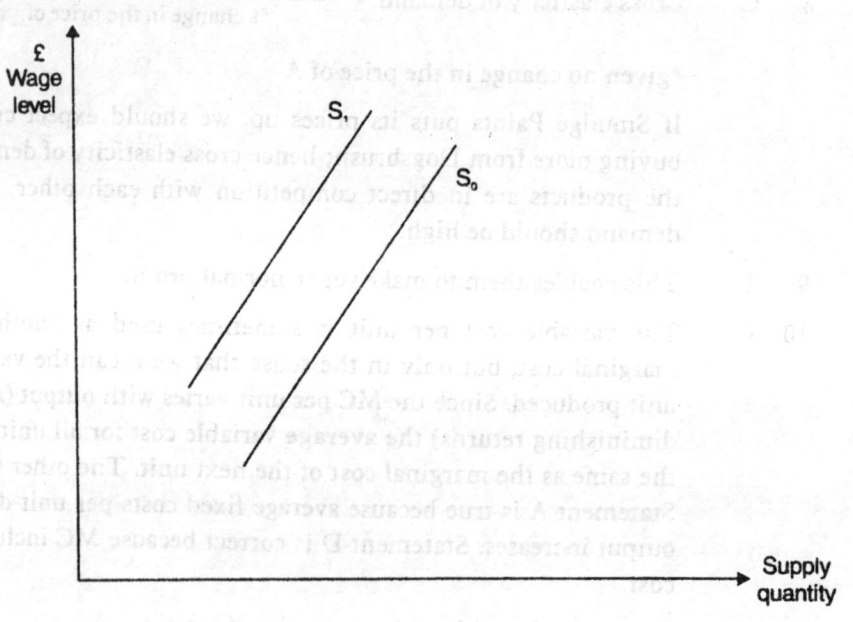

[Graph: vertical axis labelled "£ Wage level", horizontal axis labelled "Supply quantity", showing two upward sloping supply curves S_1 and S_0, with S_1 to the left of S_0.]

You must distinguish between factors which case a **shift** in the supply curve, from S_0 to S_1 (so that **any** given wage level, fewer people will offer themselves for the work) and a **movement along** the supply curve (so that fewer people will offer themselves for work if the wages offered are reduced). Item B, an increase in wages below the rate of increase in the cost of living, is a reduction in wages which will cause a movement along the supply curve. Items A, C and D will alter conditions so that there **is** a leftward shift in the supply of scientists.

16   B   Privatisation **could** mean selling off nationalised industries, but it can also refer to deregulation of industries to allow private firms to compete with state-run business (eg private bus companies) and contracting out work previously done by government employees to private firms (eg refuse collection).

Statement C is correct, and refers to the influence of 'Stock Market competition' on newly-privatised monopolies. Statement D is correct: an example in the UK is the regulatory body Oftel for BT (formerly British Telecom).

17   B   Economies of scale are possible only if there is sufficient demand for the product.

18   D   Plant and machinery are fixed factors of production, and so we are looking at the short run. Since total costs have risen by more than total output, average costs must be rising and diminishing returns are being obtained. We know nothing about revenues, and so we cannot say whether profits have risen or fallen. Average fixed costs should continue to decline as output rises, even when diminishing returns are being obtained (and AVC is rising).

Answers   Notes

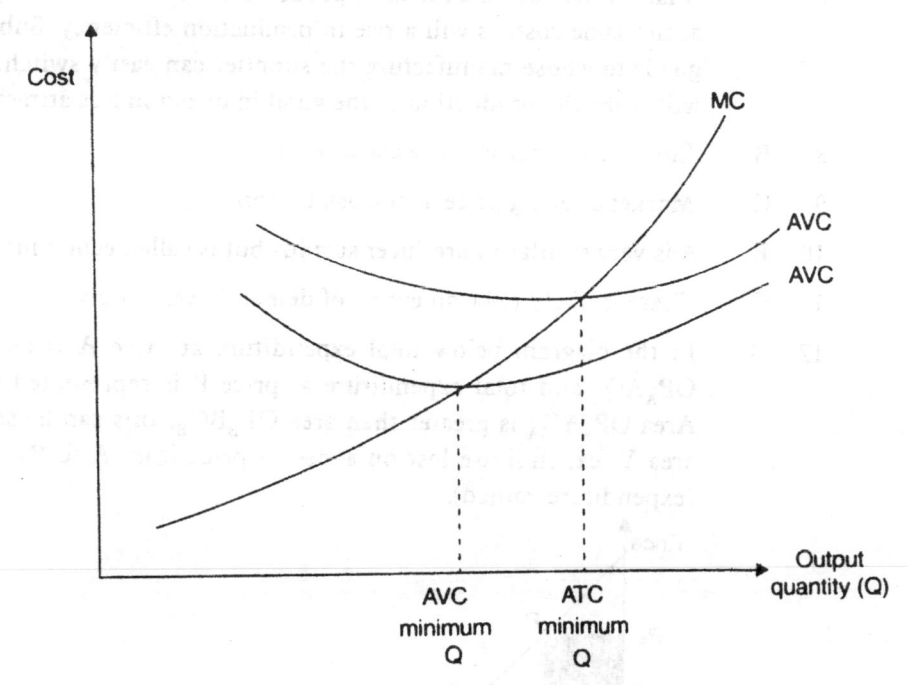

19 D

[Graph showing Cost on vertical axis and Output quantity (Q) on horizontal axis, with MC curve, AVC curve, and AVC curve (ATC). Dashed lines drop to AVC minimum Q and ATC minimum Q on the x-axis.]

20 D   Necessities of life will tend to have a low **positive** income elasticity of demand. Goods with a negative income elasticity of demand are **inferior goods**.

8   MULTIPLE CHOICE QUESTIONS

1   A   All demand other than that from households is derived demand: its magnitude and existence is derived from the ultimate household demand that firms aim to satisfy.

2   D   Marginal utility falls as consumption of the good increases. Opportunity cost is the cost of a good measured in terms of alternative foregone. Marginal cost is the extra cost incurred by producing one more unit. Economic rent of a factor of production is the element of surplus in its reward over and above its transfer earnings, the latter being the reward the factor could earn in its next best employment.

3   D   A Giffen good is one on which very poor people spend a large proportion of their income and when its price raises, their remaining income is so small that they can do nothing with it other than to buy even more of the same good. Bread is a common example. An ostentation good is one whose purchase advertises the purchaser's income and status: the higher the price, the greater the ostentation. These two types of good would have upwards sloping demand curves. The demand curve is a vertical line; hence it cannot be said to slope in either direction.

4   A   Availability of complements is an influence on demand for a good, but this is reflected in **cross-elasticity of demand**, not price elasticity of demand. Similarly, changes in household income are reflected in **income elasticity of demand**. Existence of stocks influences elasticity of **supply**.

5   C   Good A has no particular name: good B is a fashion good. Good D displays positive cross-elasticity of demand.

6   B   All actual changes in price are reflected in changes in demand by movement **along** the demand curve. Other factors such as changes in taste and *expected* price changes cause the demand curve to shift to left or right: less or more is demanded at any given price.

Notes   Answers

7   B   A fall in the cost of a factor of production will enable more goods to be produced at the same cost, as will a rise in production efficiency. Substitutes in supply are goods to whose manufacture the supplier can easily switch. A rise in their price will make the production of the good in question less attractive.

8   B   'Equilibrium price' is the usual term.

9   C   'Market clearing price' is the usual term.

10   B   A is very similar to producer surplus but is called economic rent.

11   C   There is likely to be an excess of demand over supply.

12   B   In the diagram below total expenditure at price A is represented by the area OP_AAQ_A and total expenditure at price B is represented by the area OP_BBQ_B. Area OP_AAQ_A is greater than area OP_BBQ_B: this can be seen by observing that area Y (expenditure lost on a rise in price from A to B) is greater than area X (expenditure gained).

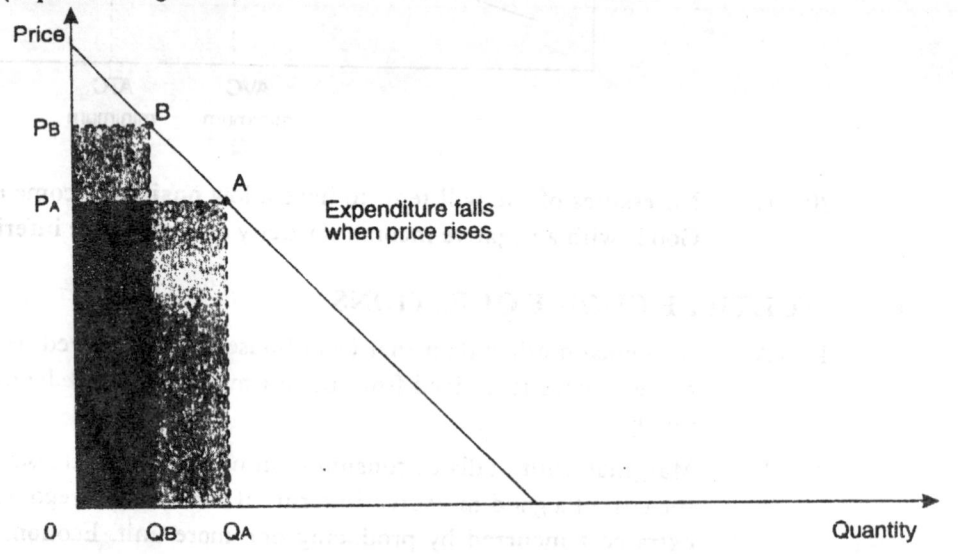

13   D   When price falls from P_B to P_A in the diagram below, quantity demanded rises from Q_B to Q_A, but total revenue, while gaining area Y, loses area X, which is much larger.

Option A is wrong: an inferior good is defined by negative income elasticity of demand. Option C is wrong: demand actually increases in quantity, as explained above. Cross-elasticity (option B) has no connection with a fall in the price of the good.

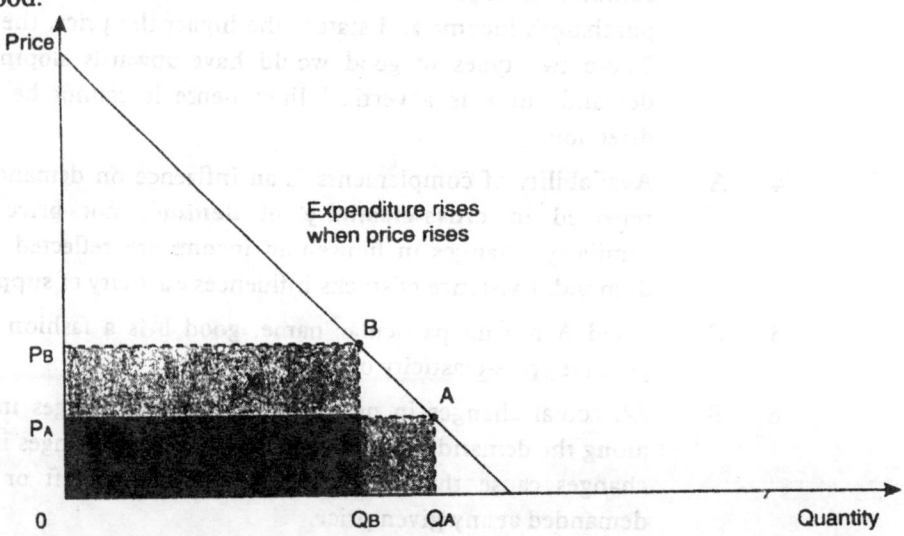

14 D Imperishability (option A) makes stockholding easier, so it becomes more likely that stocks will be available to meet an increase in demand. Low barriers to entry (option B) imply that the productive capacity of the industry can be expanded by the entry of new firms. Low unemployment (option C), however, will tend to limit the availability of skilled labour, which may in turn limit the ability of the firms in the industry to expand production. Options A and B, therefore, *both* satisfy the requirement of the question, so the correct answer is option D.

15 B Merit goods are goods that society would wish to see consumed in greater quantities than is likely under a free market system: an example is education. The other options are all true statements about perfect competition. However, note that the statement in option C about surpluses and shortages may only be true over a longer time scale, especially if extra skilled labour has to be found and complex plant built.

16 C Option A describes a **merit good**.

17 D Interest rate elasticity of demand measures the percentage change in demand for a good given a change in interest rates. When interest rates go up from 10% to 12%, the amount of the increase is 2%: confusingly perhaps, this is an increase of 0.20 or 20% of the original interest rate level of 10%. Given the high interest rate elasticity of demand for mortgage finance, there will be a fall in demand for new mortgages by over 20%. This will lead to lower demand for houses, ie a shift to the left in the demand curve for houses, and so house prices will fall.

18 C When price elasticity of demand = 1, any change in price will be matched by a change in demand quantity, so that total **revenue** (P × Q) would remain unchanged.

19 D

Old quantity	1,800	Old price	26
New quantity	1,500	New price	30
Average quantity	1,650	Average price	28
Change in quantity	300	Change in price	4
% change in quantity	18.18%	% change in price	14.29%

Elasticity $\frac{18.18}{14.29} = 1.27$

Alternatively,

Elasticity $= \frac{\text{Change in q}}{\text{Change in p}} \times \frac{(p_1 + p_2)}{(q_1 + q_2)} = \frac{300}{4} \times \frac{(26 + 30)}{(1,800 + 1,500)} = 1.27$

20 B When price elasticity of demand is zero, demand is the same regardless of price, and so yacht builders could pass on the full tax to the customer in the form of a higher price, and the equilibrium quantity sold would remain unchanged.

9 OBJECTIVE TEST QUESTIONS

1 True.

2 A decrease.

3 An increase.

4 True. Demand for inferior goods falls and demand for normal goods rises when household income rises.

Answers

5 **Point method**

% change in Q = $\frac{2}{10}$ = 20%

% change in P = $\frac{1.0}{2.5}$ = 40%

PED = $\frac{20\%}{40\%}$ = 0.5

⇒ demand is inelastic

OR $\frac{\Delta Q}{Q} \times \frac{P}{\Delta P} = \frac{2}{10} \times \frac{2.5}{1} = \frac{5}{10} = 0.5$

Arc method

$\frac{\Delta Q}{Q} \times \frac{P}{\Delta P} = \frac{2}{9} \times \frac{3}{1} = \frac{6}{9} = 0.67$

⇒ demand is inelastic

6 Fall

7 False. Demand would rise.

8 Substitutes.

9 True.

10 False. Externalities are one of the aspects of market *failure*. The term 'market imperfection' describes any market where perfect competition is not present.

11 An externality.

12 AC.

13 The demand of households.

14 False: such goods are **substitutes**; complements are bought and used together.

15 A = 3
   B = 1, 2 and 4

16 False. This may affect demand if the other goods are complements or substitutes, but not supply.

17 Consumer surplus.

18 Nil. A minimum price only leads to excess supply if it is set higher than the equilibrium price.

19 Inelastic is the correct word to describe this situation.

20 More. Consumption patterns take time to alter since it takes time for suppliers to provide substitutes and for consumers to become aware of their availability.

10 OBJECTIVE TEST QUESTIONS

1 Average variable cost: note that it cannot be average fixed cost since that declines as output increases.

2 'Above' and 'equal to' are incorrect.

3 The law of diminishing returns to scale.

4 A is marginal revenue, B is average revenue. Remember, marginal revenue can be negative.

5 Maximum.

6 False. Economies of scale are a long-run phenomenon.

7 True. This can occur when jobs are so badly paid that it is difficult to fill vacancies.

8 Elasticity of demand. If demand for the end product is inelastic, the cost of wage increase can be passed on to the end consumer but, if demand is elastic, it cannot.

9 False. Secondary sector industries manufacture goods. Service industries form the tertiary sector.

10 Homogeneous.

11 The area represents abnormal profit.

12 True. At equilibrium under perfect competition AC = MC = MR = AR.

13 Zero. The monopolist is a price maker and therefore has downward sloping average and marginal revenue curves. An increase in units sold will increase total revenue for as long as marginal revenue remains positive. MR = 0 is the limit of this process.

14 False. For price discrimination to increase profits, the separate markets must display different elasticity of demand. Otherwise the AR and MR curves are identical and there is, effectively, only one market.

15 False. Such firms are not faced with a prevailing market price because other firms' products are **comparable** rather than **homogeneous**.

16 Homogeneous; few.

17 Marginal.

18 Dead weight loss.

19 True. The fall in average fixed cost as output rises may be sufficient to outweigh a possible increase in average variable cost.

20 External. An example is the existence of a trained and experienced workforce.

11 MULTIPLE CHOICE QUESTIONS

1 A Fiscal policy is about government finance, that is, taxation, spending and borrowing.

2 A Note that interest payments are current account items.

3 D (iv) is likely to be associated with a fall in the demand for money.

4 C The bank is liable to customers for amounts deposited.

5 A This will make fixed interest investments more attractive.

6 D If there is more public borrowing, this pushes up the demand for funds and rates of interest can be expected to rise.

7 D Venture capital is a source of funds for start-up companies.

8 C A lowering of government expenditure reduces injections into the economy.

9 A The steel industry is a good UK example.

10 C Approximately.

11 C This is the definition.

12 D The PSNCR used to be called the public sector borrowing requirement.

Notes	Answers		
	13	D	Those with higher incomes are taxed proportionately more.
	14	B	The others would stimulate aggregate demand.
	15	A	Saving is a use to which income is put.
	16	D	Market forces will operate in a barter economy.
	17	D	These are **very** short term deposits. Stocks and shares change value daily. Paintings are highly illiquid.
	18	B	This specifically reduces the risk of default.
	19	B	The rate of tax paid by the business should not affect the rate charged.
	20	A	In their role as financial intermediaries.

12   MULTIPLE CHOICE QUESTIONS

	1	C	Check the definition in the BPP Study Text.
	2	B	A is 'the multiplier'.
	3	A	Securitised debt comprises tradable securities.
	4	C	This is a government role.
	5	D	Elasticity is not a meaningful concept in this context.
	6	C	As a result, money is permanently withdrawn from the circular flow, causing national income to fall.
	7	A	The transactions demand for money is said to be determined by the level of consumers' income.
	8	B	Fiscal policy relates to the government's taxation, borrowing and spending plans.
	9	A	This is a tax on externalities such as pollution.
	10	D	Investment grows faster than consumption through the action of the accelerator.
	11	B	The trade cycle concerns the rate of economic growth through time.
	12	B	Supply side economists are generally not in favour of government intervention in the economy.
	13	B	To avoid a fall in National Income, given Y = C + I + G + (X – M), a fall in G must be offset by an increase in C, I (item 3) or X (item 1).
	14	D	The other three items are all **withdrawals** from the circular flow of National Income, and so would reduce the circular flow.
	15	A	Net National Product at factor cost plus capital consumption equals Gross National Product at factor cost. By adding back taxes on expenditure and subtracting subsidies, we then get from GNP at factor cost to GNP at market prices.
	16	B	Transfer payments are payments where the recipient does not make any contribution to national output in return. They involve the transfer of wealth rather than a reward for creating economic wealth, and a redistributing of income from taxpayers to others. Salaries of Members of Parliament are a part of general government expenditure and so are included in the National Income figures.

Answers Notes

17 D   This can be written as:

$$MPC = \frac{\Delta C}{\Delta Y}$$

where C is consumption, Y is income and 'Δ' means 'change in'.

18 A   Stock building is an investment, because it involves incurring expenditures now for some benefit in the future time. Although the purchase of shares (item B), second hand machinery (item C) or an already-existing company (item D) are all investments for the individuals or organisations concerned, they are merely the transfer of ownership of already-existing assets, and there is no creation of new fixed asset capital investment or stocks. From the point of view of the national economy as a whole, these do not count as investment and do not provide an injection into the circular flow.

19 D   Increase in national income = injection $\times \frac{1}{1-MPC} = \frac{£6,000m}{0.4} = £15,000m$

20 C   Saving is good for the economy when it leads to greater investment, but higher savings without matching higher investment can lead to a fall in national income, as suggested by the so-called **paradox of thrift**.

13 MULTIPLE CHOICE QUESTIONS

1 C   Items A and B describe the multiplier effect. Item D is not correct, because although *Keynes* believed that a combination of the multiplier and the accelerator helped to cause trade cycles, this is not the accelerator principle as such. Item C correctly states that if firms have a fixed capital:output ratio, an increase in output will create a bigger proportional increase in investment in new capital equipment, so that more capital goods will be produced.

2 A   Changes in GDP can measure (and so indicate) trade cycle movements. A number of economic indicators show movements in the trade cycle, either rising (eg raw material prices) or falling (eg unemployment, bankruptcies) during a period of expansion, and the opposite during a recession. Seasonal unemployment rises or falls according to the season of the year (eg jobs for cricketers or ski instructors) and changes in this are not indicative of any business cycle movements.

3 C
	PSBR
minus	Sales of public sector debt (National Savings, gilts etc) *except such sales to the banks and building societies*
plus	Increase in bank/building society lending in sterling
plus/minus	Certain other items
equals	Increase in M4

These counterparts to the increase in M4 should suggest that anything which reduces the PSBR (now called Public Sector Net Cash Requirement) (item B) or encourages non-bank/building society lending to the government (item A) will tend to reduce the money supply. Borrowing from banks by the government (item C) has a neutral effect on the money supply. Treasury bills (item D) are short term (90 day) debt and so have no lasting effect on the money supply.

4 A   Financial intermediation is the process of taking deposits from customers and re-lending to borrowers (at a higher rate of interest). Item B could refer to a firm of 'market makers'. Item C refers to a leasing company or finance house. Item D refers to the former role of the discount houses.

Notes	Answers		
5	C	Customers' deposits are **liabilities** of a bank, not assets. The assets of a typical retail bank include notes and coin (till money), and near-liquid assets such as deposits with money market institutions (eg inter-bank loans), bills of exchange and certificates of deposit (CDs). Most of the asset of a retail bank are their loans and overdrafts to customers. (Operational assets such as buildings and equipment are very small in value compared to a bank's financial assets).	
6	D	Since $MV = PT$, $V = \dfrac{PT}{M}$	
		This is described by item D. Item A is incorrect because it states that $V = M \div P$ and item C is incorrect because it states that $V = PT \div P$.	
7	B	According to Keynes the money supply could be fixed by the authorities. The demand for money depends on three motives (transactions, precautionary and speculative) but it is the speculative demand for money that is sensitive to changes in interest rates, and this explains the liquidity preference schedule.	
8	C	Higher value added tax, which is a sales tax, will make goods more expensive to buy. Consumers will need more money to pay for them, and so their transactions demand for money will rise.	
9	C	Higher wages result in higher output costs per unit (unless labour productivity improved to compensate for the higher wages). This leads to firms having to raise their prices and so to cost-push inflation. Higher import prices, whether raw materials for industry, capital goods for industry or consumer goods, lead to import-cost-push inflation. Factor 2 is a cause of demand-pull inflation.	
10	B	This calls for a straightforward definition of frictional unemployment. Item A is a cause of structural unemployment and item D causes seasonal unemployment. Item C refers to demand-deficient unemployment	
11	D	The monetarists argue that **inflation** should be brought under control by keeping the growth in the money supply under control. They also argue that lower unemployment is achievable without higher inflation (which would normally happen, with the Phillips curve effect) by reducing the natural rate of unemployment or 'non-accelerating inflation rate of unemployment' (NAIRU). This can be done by 'supply side' measures, such as reducing incentives for individuals to be unemployed (eg cutting welfare benefits) and reducing income tax rates to give individuals a bigger incentive to work more to earn more money.	
12	D	A progressive tax is one in which individuals on higher income pay a greater proportion of their income in tax. Hugh earns twice as much as Howard but pays 2½ times as much income. Hymie earns 50% more than Hugh but pays over twice as much in income tax.	
13	B	GNP at factor cost is calculated by removing taxes on expenditure, such as sales tax or value added tax.	

14	A		2001	2002
			$ million	$ million
		Consumers' expenditure	200,000	225,000
		Government expenditure	70,000	74,000
		Fixed capital formation	54,000	60,000
			324,000	359,000
		Exports	93,000	94,000
		Imports	(92,000)	(99,000)
		GDP at market prices	325,000	354,000

Answers Notes

$$\text{Increase } (354 - 325) = \$29,000 \text{ million}$$
$$\text{\% increase in money terms} = \frac{29,000}{325,000} \times 100\% = 8.9\%$$

% change in real terms, with 10% inflation, is a fall of about 1%

15 D   Capital consumption represents an estimated cost based on **current prices** for the gradual using up of the nation's productive fixed assets. It is difficult to estimate accurately. Statement A is incorrect, largely because inter-country comparisons of living standards would be based on National Income per **head** rather than total National Income. Statement B is incorrect because services provided free such as policing are included in the statistics at actual cost. Statement C is wrong because when there is a strong black economy, with economic activity not reported to the government to avoid taxation, official statistics will **underestimate** National Income.

16 B   An inflationary gap exists when there is full employment, and aggregate demand exceeds the ability of the economy to produce output, and so prices rise. An inflationary gap is closed by increasing the physical output capacity of the economy, or by reducing aggregate demand. Item B does this, because a bigger surplus of taxation income over government spending reduces aggregate demand.

17 D   Remember the multiplier formula! The marginal propensity to import (m) and the marginal rate of taxation (t) help to reduce the size of the multiplier, in addition to the marginal propensity to save (s).

18 A   When an economy booms, it reaches a turning point and goes into recession, the recession deepens into a depression. Eventually, there is another turning point in the economy, and the business cycle goes into recovery and then back into boom, and so on.

19 C   If the banks maintained a 10% cash ratio, the credit multiplier for any initial increase in cash deposit will be 1/10% = 10 times.

Maximum increase in bank deposits = £1 million × 5 banks × 10 (credit multiplier)
                                  = £50 million

However, this £50 million includes the initial deposits of £5 million, and so the **further** increase in total bank deposits is £50 million − £5 million = £45 million.

20 B   The solution can be shown by algebra. The extra cash deposited with the banks (£C) is already a part of the money supply, and so using the credit multiplier formula, we have:

$$\frac{C}{20\%} = 300 + C$$
$$C = 20\% (300 + C)$$
$$0.8C = 60$$
$$C = 75$$

If £75 million extra is deposited with banks, the total volume of deposits or cash (ie the money supply) will rise to £75 million ÷ 20% = £375 million. This includes the initial £75 million, and so the money supply will increase by £300 million. (A temptation might have been to give answer A here).

Notes   **Answers**

14   MULTIPLE CHOICE QUESTIONS

1 D Maturity transformation is a feature of the role of financial intermediaries, such as building societies and banks. Item B describes 'redemption value'. Item C is sometimes described as a yield curve.

2 D Nominal rate of interest = Real rate of interest + Rate of inflation (approx) = 3% + 6% = 9%.

3 D T has to be unchanged for the equation MV = PT to be a predictor of price behaviour. Any increase in M, given no change in V in the short tun, would result in a matching percentage increase in prices P.

4 A Lower interest rates should be a consequence of an increase in the money supply, with a movement along the liquidity preference curve rather than a shift in the liquidity preference curve (item B).

5 A Items B, C and D will all be measures which reduce the demand for goods and services. Public expenditure (item D) represents the government's own demand. Bank lending (item C) is largely used for spending on goods and services by the people who borrow the money. Higher value added tax (item B) could increase total spending on goods and services **inclusive** of the tax, but spending **net** of tax will fall, and this should result in a reduction in demand-pull inflation. Item A, lower interest rates, is likely to result in higher consumer borrowing and even stronger demand-pull inflation.

6 D Keynes' analysis of inflation considered the situation where aggregate demand exceeded the ability of the economy to produce real output to meet the demand, resulting in demand-pull inflation and an inflationary gap.

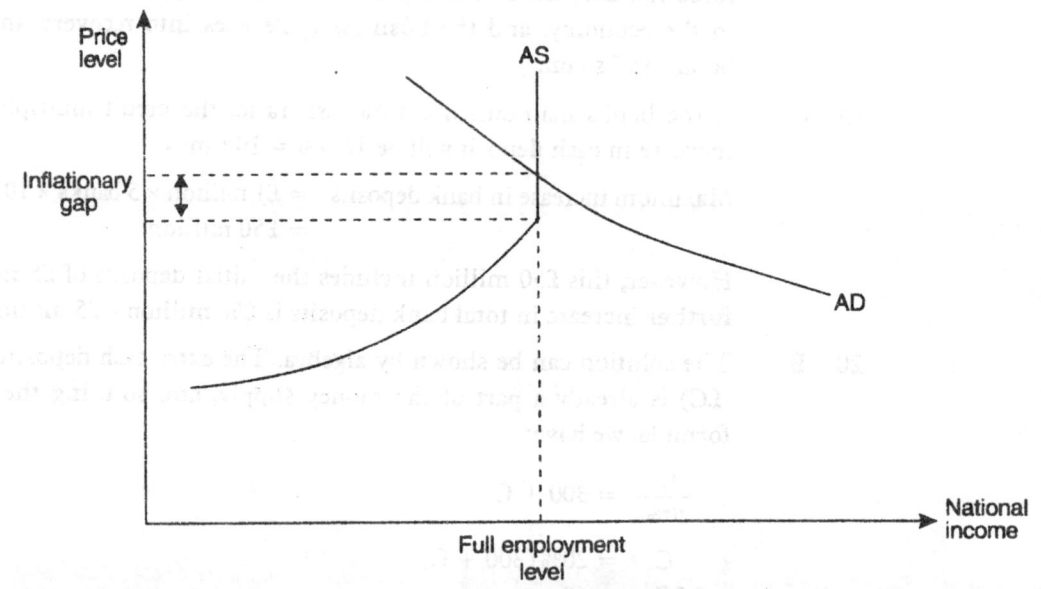

7 D The RPI attempts to measure the cost of living and the rate of inflation. If the index goes up, prices have gone up, there has been some inflation, and so the value of money has fallen. The **standard** of living might have gone up or down, depending on changes in incomes, but the RPI does not measure this (National Income per capita is a better measure for item A). The RPI has gone up by 4%, but the increase in wages needed to keep pace with this will depend on other factors too, such as income tax rates and so item B is not correct. Item C is incorrect, because to analyse changes in the RPI, we assume that consumption patterns have remained much the same.

8	C	Structural unemployment is caused by a mismatch between available jobs and the unemployed. This could be caused by a geographical mismatch (eg jobs available in London and unemployed people in Liverpool) or by a mismatch of skills (eg unemployed labourers, job vacancies for skilled workers in electronics). Items B and D could be **causes** of structural unemployment, but don't fully describe it.
9	A	Freidman argued that stimulating demand will only have a temporary effect on unemployment, and that demand-led expansion of the economy would soon become inflationary (with no increase in the real output). He argued in favour of supply side measures to reduce the natural rate of unemployment. Retraining schemes (item B) should reduce structural unemployment. Cutting trade union power (item C) was seen as a way of reducing unemployment. Lower income taxes (item D) and lower benefits for the unemployed would make individuals more willing to work and less willing to remain unemployed.
10	A	A flat-rate poll tax, with no concession for the lower-paid, would take a higher proportion of the income of lower-income earners than of higher-income earners. Taxes that have this effect are regressive taxes. Television licences and road tax for cars are other examples.
11	D	A reduction in taxes on alcoholic drinks will leave all consumers of alcohol with more income. A less even distribution of wealth in society means that richer people will now be relatively better off than before, which means that they have obtained a bigger benefit from the tax cuts. The conclusion points to either answer B or answer D. The benefit has to be **relative**, since the distribution of wealth refers to relative (proportionate) wealth, and so answer D must be correct.
12	C	The opportunity cost of leisure will fall if fewer goods and services can be bought with income earned from working. An **increase** in the rate of tax on income or on goods that can be bought with income will have this effect, and so item C is correct. A poll tax will presumably be levied on all individuals, working or not working, and so does not alter the opportunity cost of working. Similarly, a capital transfer tax does not have a direct bearing on the opportunity cost of working, because it is only applied when individuals transfer wealth to each other, not when income is earned from working.
13	B	A revaluation of the currency (item A) should make import costs cheaper. An increase in direct taxation (item B) will not reduce pressures for higher costs; if anything, it will encourage workers to demand higher wages, which will add to cost-push inflationary pressures. Wage drift (item C) is the tendency for annual wages increases to run ahead of the rate of inflation and to 'drift' upwards, and controlling this would reduce inflationary pressures from higher costs. Linking wage and salary increases to productivity improvements (item D) will help to keep unit costs down, and so reduce cost-push inflationary pressures.
14	C	Employers' National Insurance contributions are paid by firms to the government for each of their employees. A reduction in these contributions will, in effect, reduce the cost of labour. Lower wages costs will increase the demand for labour by firms. Higher VAT, a higher budget surplus and lower spending on nationalised industries (items A, B and D) would all reduce spending/demand in the economy, and so should be expected to **increase** the level of unemployment.
15	D	Fiscal policy is concerned with the government' tax income, expenditure and borrowing (to make up the difference between income and expenditure.
16	C	It is aggregate supply in the economy which is at issue.

17	D	Higher taxation will tend to reduce consumer spending. Higher import tariffs might result in greater consumer expenditure on imports inclusive of tariffs, but the volume and the net-of-tariff value of imports purchased will fall. Higher social security payments will give consumers more cash to spend.
18	A	Recession and declining demand go together. Inflation and declining demand do not.
19	A	A rise in cyclical unemployment is a consequence of a fall in the level of economic activity rather than its cause
20	B	The retail banks primarily take deposits and make loans in the retail market.

15 OBJECTIVE TEST QUESTIONS

1. Structural.

2. Frictional and cyclical are incorrect.

3. False. Structural unemployment is best tackled by supply side measures. Demand management can only affect demand-deficient (cyclical) unemployment.

4. A = inflation
   B = unemployment

5. NAIRU

6. False. If interest rates rise investment will be attracted from other countries. This will increase the demand for sterling causing the exchange rate to rise. This, in turn, will make exports more expensive.

7. False. The correct name is **demand pull** inflation.

8. Prices will rise by 5%.

9. False. Expectational inflation arises when **wage claims** incorporate an element to cover future price rises. A rise in interest rates will tend to reduce inflation by reducing the rate of credit creation and hence the volume of demand.

10. True. The market price falls until the fixed interest income equates to the rate of income.

11. False. This is what the accelerator principle does.

12. Net property income from abroad.

13. $\Delta NI = \dfrac{\Delta J}{1 - MPC}$

    $= \dfrac{£4bn}{1 - 0.8}$

    $= £20bn$

14. Keynes argues that **an increase** in the money supply would lead to lower interest rates.

15. A, C Higher interest rates should discourage consumer spending with borrowed money and spending on credit. Higher interest rates should **attract** investors into sterling. They should also discourage borrowing, and since borrowing from banks and building societies is the main cause of increases in the broad money supply, there should be some **slowing down** of money supply growth.

16 OBJECTIVE TEST QUESTIONS

1.
    A 3
    B 4
    C 5
    D 1
    E 2

2. False. Exports are an injection.

3. Net property income from abroad.

4. Capital consumption.

5. Y2.

6. It is an inflationary gap.

7. True. Poor households have a higher propensity to consume since they need most of their income to pay for subsistence.

8. $\Delta NI = \dfrac{\Delta J}{1 - MPC}$

    $= \dfrac{£2bn}{1 - 0.9}$

    $= £20bn$

9. False. The accelerator principle helps to explain the existence of the business cycle by showing how investment changes **disproportionately** in response to changes in consumption.

10. Right to left. Employment falls and prices rise.

11. False. Banks operate the credit multiplier by holding fractional reserves; compulsory minimum deposits at the central bank are intended to reduce their credit creation ability.

12. False. The tax revenue stabiliser effect arises from tax revenues that **rise** as national income rises.

13. Fiscal drag.

14. True. It is levied at a flat rate, and bears more heavily on those with low incomes.

15. False. The poverty trap exists because welfare benefits are withdrawn if earnings increase. An increase in earnings thus may produce no benefit. Indeed, if a tax threshold is crossed, the person concerned may be worse off.

16. False. This is part of the significance of the **Laffer** curve. The Phillips curve is concerned with unemployment and inflation.

17. False. Inflation distributes wealth from creditors to debtors. This is unlikely to be a transfer from rich to poor.

18. Precautionary

19. 'Higher' is incorrect.

20. True. AD will rise, leading to inflation.

Notes   Answers

17 MULTIPLE CHOICE QUESTIONS

1   B   A and D are benefits of fixed exchange rates; C does not apply to any exchange rate system.

2   C   Opportunity cost is the key to understanding comparative advantage.

3   D   Tariffs allow domestic producers to raise their prices.

4   C   It sometimes seems that *anything* can contribute to pressure on fixed exchange rates, but changes in unemployment are unlikely to do so. A case might be made for suggesting that falling unemployment might herald cost push inflation which might in turn put downward pressure on an exchange rate.

5   B   The theory is founded on opportunity cost.

6   D   A single currency requires a single monetary policy.

7   D   This statement is nonsense.

8   A   The expenditure to be reduced in this context is expenditure on imports. A will tend to do this by deflating the economy.

9   C   D is likely to follow after C.

10 B   This is the only one likely to boost import demand.

11 A   B and D are characteristic of fixed exchange rates. C can only happen with a common currency; however, a fixed exchange rate can eliminate the costs associated with managing exchange rate risk, such as the cost of hedging.

12 C   This is the usual description. Not all EU, EEA or EFTA countries use the euro.

13 C   The terms of trade relate import and export prices.

14 B   Financing a deficit requires **foreign** currency.

15 A   This would apply to **all** goods, whether imported or not.

16 D   Note that the question asks about **capital** markets.

17 A   This is a problem for government management of international trade and the balance of payments.

18 D   A point of definition.

19 B   This will tend to increase the unit value of exports.

20 C   Country X has an **absolute** advantage over Country Y in making P and Q, because 1 unit of resource in Country X will make more of either P or Q than one unit of resource in Country Y. However, international trade should still take place because of **comparative** advantage in producing P and Q.

The opportunity costs of producing a unit of P is ($4/8$) = $1/2$ unit of Q in Country X and only $1/3$ unit of Q in Country Y.

Similarly, the opportunity cost of producing a unit of Q is 2 units of P in Country X and 3 units of P in Country Y.

Country X has a comparative advantage in producing P and Country Y has a comparative advantage in the production of Q. International trade should be beneficial for both countries, with Country X exporting P and Country Y exporting Q.

18 MULTIPLE CHOICE QUESTIONS

1 A To Bandia, the opportunity cost of producing 1 tonne of rice is $1/15$ car and the opportunity cost of making a car is 15 tonnes of rice.

To Sparta, the opportunity cost of producing rice is higher than in Bandia, because it is $1/6$ car. the opportunity cost of making a car is less, because it is just 6 tonnes of rice.

Since Bandia has a comparative advantage over Sparta in producing rice and Sparta has a comparative advantage over Bandia in making cars, international trade will occur, with Bandia exporting rice and Sparta exporting cars.

2 C

	Unit value of exports		Unit value of imports				Terms of trade
Base year	100	÷	100	×	100	=	100
Current level	108	÷	120	×	100	=	90

3 A The terms of trade are not an item in the Balance of Payments figures. All the other items represent capital movements between the UK and abroad, and would be reported as increases or decreases in UK external assets and liabilities.

4 C The balance of payments is in deficit when there is a deficit on the combined visible and invisible balance. Capital movements are not included, and so item 2 is irrelevant. The invisible balance includes services such as **tourism** (item 1). British tourism abroad creates an outflow and has an adverse effect on the balance of payments. **Transfers** as an item of invisible trade includes such items as payments by the UK government to the European community and the United Nations, and cash grants to developing countries (item 3).

5 C If real incomes rise in the UK, spending in the UK economy would rise. Some of this extra spending would be on imports.

6 B 'Balance of payments' in the question refers to balance of payment on current account. Capital movements (Reason 2) do not have a short-term effect on the balance of payments, although in the longer term, there will be outflows of interest and dividend payments to the foreign investors.

When an economy is reflated, the government will take steps to increase aggregate demand. Some of this extra demand will be satisfied by imported goods (Reason 3) and some by domestically-produced goods. Unless industry has sufficient spare capacity to meet the extra domestic demand and also to carry on producing for the same volume of exports as before, the growth in domestic demand will result in some switch by firms from selling to export market to selling to domestic markets (Reason 1).

7 C A conclusion from the law of comparative advantage is that if free trade is allowed, countries will specialise in the production of goods and services in which they have a comparative advantage over other countries. As a result, the world's economic resources will be put to their most productive uses, and total output will be maximised. It does not follow that each country of the world will maximise its own National Income of economic wealth (Statement A), because the distribution of the wealth between the individual countries in the world could be uneven, with some countries earning much more than others from their output and their exports.

8 D In both countries, the opportunity cost of producing wheat is $1/3$ unit of beef, and the opportunity cost of producing beef is 3 units of wheat. Since neither country

Notes   Answers

therefore has a comparative advantage over the other in producing wheat or beef, neither can benefit economically from international trade.

9   D   The balance of **trade** refers to the export and import of visible goods, and does **not** refer to invisible items such as tourism and services. Only item 3, which consists of both imports and exports of visible items, would be included in the balance of trade figures.

10 C   This is just one example of how a country's terms of trade might improve. By switching from low-priced to high-priced products in a major export industry unit export prices will go up and the terms of trade will improve. The change in the **balance** of trade depends on changes in the **volume** of exports and imports **as well as change in export and import prices.**

11 C   Investment in the UK by foreign firms is a capital transaction and does not affect the balance of payments on current account. items A, B and D are all items that will be included in the invisible section of the current account.

12 D   **Reason 1.** with domestic inflation, export prices will go up. Total exports in value might go up or down, depending on the price elasticity of demand for exports. However, higher export prices would improve the terms of trade, not weaken them.

Reason 2. High prices for domestically produced goods will increase demand for (substitute) imported goods, and so add to total imports.

Reason 3. If inflation is caused by excess demand in domestic markets, firms will produce goods for their domestic market, and not have the output capacity to export as well. We might say that output has been 'diverted' from export markets to domestic markets, so that total exports will fall in value.

13 A   This is a straightforward definition question. Reserve currencies are currencies that are used by governments and international institutions for holding their official reserves.

14 D   Devaluation of the currency will make imports more expensive. The price of exports should not be directly affected by the devaluation, and so the terms of trade (unit value of exports ÷ unit value of imports) will worsen. Higher costs of imports will add to the cost of living.

15 D   The price of exports will have risen relative to the price of imports, but (a) the balance of payments on current account might either improve or worsen, depending on the price elasticities of demand for exports and imports (b) the exchange rate is dependent on supply and demand for the currency, arising from capital movements and the balance of payments – and is not dependent on changes in the terms of trade, and (c) the terms of trade can improve **either** when export prices go up **or** when import prices fall, and so an improvement in the terms of trade is not **necessarily** a consequence of higher export prices.

16 D   Exchange rates in the foreign exchange markets are determined by the interaction of demand and supply. An excessive outflow of sterling from the UK means either that there are large capital outflows or that there are large outflows caused by a balance of payments deficit. This will create an extra supply of sterling for sale in the foreign exchange markets, and the price of sterling, which is the exchange rate for sterling against other traded currencies, would fall.

17 C   With a depreciation in the value of sterling, import prices rise, because it costs more in £ sterling to obtain the foreign currency to pay foreign suppliers for the imported goods. Since demand for imports is inelastic, the fall in demand for

imports resulting from an increase in their price will be relative small, and total spending on imports will rise.

18   D   **Consequence 3.** Depreciation of the currency will make imports more expensive. For a country with high imports relative to the size of its national Income, this is likely to lead to some import-cost-push inflation.

Consequence 2. If demand for imports is inelastic, the increase in import prices will result in an increase in total spending on imports. Exports will be cheaper to foreign buyers, and even if demand is inelastic, total exports will rise in volume and in value. However, with imports increasing and exports increase by only a little, the balance of trade will worsen.

Consequence 1. with imports prices rising after the depreciation, the terms of trade will **worsen.**

19   C   When a currency appreciates in value, imports become cheaper to buy but exports become more expensive for foreign buyers. Demand for imports is price inelastic, and so a fall in the price of imports will result in a fall in total spending on imports. Exports prices in Gerdaland's own currency will be unchanged, but prices to foreign buyers will go up. Higher export prices to foreign buyers will result in a fall in total export volumes and so in total export revenue for Gerdaland.

20   D   Higher interest rates should attract more investments from abroad into the country and so there will be **capital inflows** into the country. The capital inflows should cause an **appreciation in the currency,** because foreign investors must buy the currency to pay for their investments in the country. With an appreciation in the currency, imports become cheaper to buy and exports become more expensive to foreign buyers. With inelastic demand, this means that total spending on imports will fall. The volume of exports will fall, and so total revenue from exports in the exporter's **domestic current domestic currency** will fall too. (Total spending by foreign buyers on exports will rise, but only in their own currency.)

19   MULTIPLE CHOICE QUESTIONS

1   D

	Unit value of exports	Unit value of imports		Terms of trade
19X2	106	÷ 112	× 100	= 94.64
19X3	114	÷ 116	× 100	= 98.28

Improvement (increase in index) = $\frac{98.28 - 94.64}{94.64}$ = 0.038 or 3.8 approx.

2   B   The data shows the visible balance and the invisible balance, which are the difference between exports and imports of goods (visible balance) and between earnings and payments for services, interest profit and dividends and transfers (invisible balance). The improvement in these balances in 19X8 compared with 19X1 could have been caused by falling imports rather than rising exports.

3   D   The current balance is simply the visible balance plus the invisible balance, and 18 + 7 = 25.

4   D   The balance of payments for 19X8 will be as follows.

Notes   Answers

	£'000 million	£'000 million
Current balance		+25
Transactions in external assets		
Investment abroad	−27	
Lending abroad	−30	
Additions to official reserves	−2	
		−59
Transactions in external liabilities		
Investing from abroad	12	
Borrowing from abroad	25	
		37
		−22
Balancing item		−3
		−25

5 A   See previous answer.

6 B   When the US dollar depreciates against the euro, but maintains its value against sterling, it follows that sterling will depreciate against the euro too. When sterling and the US dollar depreciate in value, UK and US goods become cheaper for countries in the euro zone to buy. The relative prices of UK and US goods will remains the same as before, and so US goods will not change in price in the UK (and UK goods will not change in price in the USA).

7 D   Note that the common currency's exchange rates may fluctuate widely.

8 A   The others do not.

9 B   **Changes** in the levels of overseas investment are capital flows and **do** affect the exchange rate

10 D   The budget deficit is a matter of government financing.

11 B   Patent protections would not be reduced.

12 C   A customs union is essentially a free trade area with common external tariffs.

13 D   The export of capital will increase the demand for foreign currency, putting downward pressure on the domestic currency.

14 B   Imports priced in foreign currency would be more expensive since a greater amount of domestic currency would be needed to pay for them.

15 D   These are the products it produces most efficiently.

16 C   Capital is **highly** mobile.

17 C   Existing low wage economies will experience increasing demand for their labour. Their average wage will therefore rise.

18 A   Definition.

19 D   A has no particular name. B and C are both called the balance of trade.

20 A   Import quotas reduce the supply of imports: the prices of those imports therefore tend to rise.

20   OBJECTIVE TEST QUESTIONS

1   False. This describes **absolute** advantage.

2   Guns. It has to give up 15 tons of butter to produce one gun domestically, but it can obtain one from Country Y in exchange for only 10 tons of butter.

Answers Notes

3 False. 'Dumping' is exporting goods at less than a fair cost in order to support domestic industry.

4 False. This may be useful but it is not essential.

5 Increase. Extra supply of anything tends to lead to a falling price.

6 True. The country with the higher exchange rate will eventually be forced to devalue.

7 Decrease. There will be increased need to buy foreign currency to pay for imports: demand for foreign currency will go up, demand for sterling will go down.

8 B, C and D all apply.

9 Surplus is incorrect. A rise in interest rates will lead to a rise in the exchange rate. This will make exports more expensive and imports cheaper, thus causing the balance of trade to deteriorate.

10 A Current account balance
   B Time

11 True.

12 False. The J curve effect is a short run phenomenon.

13 Decrease. It is widely accepted that the current sterling/euro exchange is too high and that a fall would be engineered before entry.

14 False. Volumes of imports and exports must also be considered.

15 Exchange.

16 180 $\dfrac{2003 \text{ exports index}/2002 \text{ exports index}}{2003 \text{ imports index}/2002 \text{ imports index}} = 0.8$

$\dfrac{144/150}{216/x} = 0.8$

$144/150 = 0.8 \left(\dfrac{216}{x}\right)$

$\dfrac{144/150}{0.8} = \dfrac{216}{x}$

$x = \dfrac{216 \times 0.8}{144/150}$

17 Monetary. Member nations retain control over fiscal policy, though there are limitations on their freedom of action.

18 False. Import prices can rise because of scarcity.

19 'Reduce' is incorrect.

20 True.

21 **MULTIPLE CHOICE QUESTIONS**

1 D This might increase the number of people in the labour force but would not increase its productivity. Indeed, it would probably reduce it since these marginal workers would tend to include the least able and the least motivated.

2 D Diseconomies of scale are a long run effect. The long run cost curve does not necessarily rise once MES has been reached. X inefficiency is a failure of cost control.

109

3	C	Draw a simple supply and demand diagram.	
4	A	The other options all deal with less basic problems.	
5	B	Draw the diagrams.	
6	C	Market failure is an economic term, not a political one.	
7	B	C is tempting but note that prices will be 'sticky' in an oligopoly whether or not there is collusion.	
8	A	This is a fundamental point.	
9	D	All resources are scarce. B is about the balance of payments rather than social welfare. C is irrelevant.	
10	C	The effect of a fall in price is shown by the demand curve as it stands.	
11	B	A and C are incomplete statements. D is very loosely concerned with the difference between GDP at market prices and GDP at factor cost.	
12	B	This is the mechanism by which D is achieved.	
13	A	The reverse of this statement is true.	
14	D	A and C are seasonal unemployment; B is structural unemployment.	
15	C	The theory predicts that the purchasing power of different currencies should equate, over time. A Big Mac in Tokyo should cost the same as a Big Mac in London, according to the theory.	
16	A	This is a point of definition.	
17	B	Unemployment would only fall if the increased after-tax income were used for consumption.	
18	B	A contractionary policy is likely to cause after-tax incomes to fall.	
19	D	A point of definition.	
20	C	This is the basic conclusion from the idea of comparative advantage.	

22 MULTIPLE CHOICE QUESTIONS

1	C	This would require production to be concentrated.
2	D	Factors will be attracted to places where their price is highest. The resulting increase in supply will cause the price to fall. Eventually price differentials will be minimised.
3	B	There is a tendency to break up the manufacturing process in order to exploit small differences of comparative and absolute advantage.
4	B	Taxation is reserved to national governments in a common market.
5	A	B, C and D would have the opposite effect.
6	A	C and D would reduce the availability of labour. B would merely employ more of the existing resource.
7	C	Definition.
8	D	This is a boost to aggregate demand.
9	C	Monopoly and oligopoly are market forms.
10	B	Fact.

11 B Current revenue = 10,000 × $10 = $100,000

$$\text{Elasticity} = \frac{\%\Delta Q}{\%\Delta P}$$

$$-2.5 = \frac{\%\Delta Q}{10\%}$$

⇒ %ΔQ = −0.25

⇒ new volume = 10,000 − 2,500

7,500 @ $11 = $82,500

∴ revenue change is a reduction of $17,000

Plausibility check: −2.5 is a rather high value for elasticity, therefore a fall in revenue is correct.

12 D Fact.

13 A B, C and D are legal barriers.

14 B As opposed to a public good, whose consumption by one group does not preclude consumption by others and from whose consumption it is difficult to exclude people.

15 A Fact.

16 D The monopolist's power depends on controlling total output.

17 C This does not directly affect those not party to the transaction.

18 C Prices may be supported above their equilibrium level as with the EU Common Agricultural Policy.

19 D This would reduce the volume of money circulated from an initial injection.

20 B Fact.

11. B   Current revenue = 10,000 × $10 = $100,000

$$\text{Elasticity} = \frac{\%\Delta Q}{\%\Delta P}$$

$$-2.5 = \frac{\%\Delta Q}{10\%}$$

$$\%\Delta Q = -0.25$$

new volume = 10,000 − 2,500

7,500 in $11 = $82,500

∴ revenue change is a reduction of $17,500

Plausibility check: −2.5 is a rather high value for elasticity, therefore a fall in revenue is correct.

12. D   Fact.

13. A   B, C and D are legal barriers.

14. B   As opposed to a public good, whose consumption by one group does not preclude consumption by others and from whose consumption it is difficult to exclude people.

15. A   Fact.

16. D   The monopolist's power depends on controlling total output.

17. C   Tax does not directly affect above-the-line or the transaction.

18. C   Prices may be supposed above their equilibrium levels with the EU Common Agricultural Policy.

19. D   This would increase the volume of money required from an initial injection.

112

Foundation

MOCK ASSESSMENT 1

Paper 3a

Economics for Business

FECB

| You are allowed one hour to answer this assessment. |
| Answer ALL questions. |

**DO NOT OPEN THIS PAPER UNTIL YOU ARE READY
TO START UNDER EXAMINATION CONDITIONS**

1   In all economies, the fundamental economic problem is that:

    A   consumers never have as much money as they would wish
    B   resources are scarce relative to human wants
    C   there is always some unemployment of resources
    D   the supply of resources is always less than the demand for them

2   Which ONE of the following is NOT a cost of production for a firm?

    A   Salaries of senior managers
    B   Normal profit
    C   Interest payable on loans
    D   Corporation tax

3   If the demand for a good is *price inelastic*, then the total expenditure on the good:

    A   will fall if the price rises
    B   will be constant if the price rises
    C   will rise if the price rises
    D   will rise if the price falls

4   All of the following would lead firms in an industry to locate close together in one area EXCEPT which ONE?

    A   A local supply of raw materials
    B   Specialist training facilities located in the area
    C   The opportunity for external economies of scale
    D   The existence of a cartel in the industry

5   A profit-maximising firm will attempt to produce where:

    A   marginal cost is equal to marginal revenue
    B   average costs of production are lowest
    C   marginal cost equals average cost
    D   marginal cost is equal to average revenue

6   Which ONE of the following is an example of price discrimination?

    A   A bus company charging a lower price than a railway company for the same distance travelled
    B   A telecommunications company charging reduced rates for telephone calls made by government bodies
    C   Supermarkets charging different prices for fruit in different regions because local supply costs vary
    D   Petrol stations charging lower prices for unleaded petrol than for leaded petrol

7   All of the following are characteristics of oligopolies EXCEPT which ONE?

    A   There is a small number of firms in the industry
    B   There is a preference for non-price competition
    C   There is very little product differentiation
    D   There are entry barriers to the industry

Mock assessment 1

8   Monopolies are undesirable because they:

    A   control most of the market
    B   maximise profits
    C   do not pass on to consumers the benefits of economies of scale
    D   do not produce where average costs are lowest

9   Many building societies are now performing functions which are increasingly similar to commercial banks in that they now:

    A   pay interest on all their deposit accounts
    B   have more branches than many banks
    C   provide full cheque accounts and money transfer services
    D   have a significantly greater level of deposits than banks

10   Which ONE of the following is the most *profitable* to a commercial bank?

    A   Advances to customers
    B   Balances with the central bank
    C   Money at call
    D   Treasury Bills

11   Which of the following are functions of money?

    (i)   A medium of exchange
    (ii)   A store of value
    (iii)   A unit of account
    (iv)   A measure of liquidity

    A   (i) and (ii) only
    B   (i), (ii) and (iii) only
    C   (ii), (iii) and (iv) only
    D   All of them

12   Which ONE of the following is a transfer payment in national income accounting?

    A   Educational scholarships
    B   Salaries of lecturers
    C   Payments for textbooks
    D   Payments of examination entry fees

13   Which of the following would increase the potential benefits from international trade?

    (i)   The existence of economies of scale in production
    (ii)   A high mobility of capital and labour between economies
    (iii)   Large differences in the opportunity costs of production between countries
    (iv)   Low international transport costs

    A   (i), (ii) and (iii) only
    B   (ii), (iii) and (iv) only
    C   (i), (iii) and (iv) only
    D   All of them

14 All of the following would raise the demand for imports in a country except which one?

  A A rise in consumer incomes
  B A reduction in tariffs
  C A rise in the domestic price level
  D A devaluation of the exchange rate

15 Consider the supply of yachts. Just recently, the price of sailcloth has fallen substantially. The supply of yachts is perfectly inelastic in the short term. What would happen in the short term?

  A The equilibrium supply quantity and price of yachts would be unchanged
  B The supply curve for yachts would shift to the right, and the price of sailing yachts would fall. More yachts would be made and sold
  C The supply curve for yachts would shift to the right, and the price of sailing yachts would fall. The same quantity of yachts as before would be made and sold.
  D The supply curve for yachts would be unchanged, and the quantity made would be the same as before. However, their price would fall, with cost savings being passed on to the customer

16 Holden Tite is a professional footballer, playing in goal for his team. He earns a wage which is more than sufficient to keep him in his job, and the excess income he earns is called:

  A Opportunity cost
  B Economic rent
  C Transfer earnings
  D Surplus value

17 Which of the following statement is *not* true about the price mechanism?

  A Monopoly and other restrictive practices obstruct the smooth re-allocation of resources
  B In a private enterprise system, the sovereignty of the consumer is complete
  C Immobility of factors makes the price mechanism less efficient as an allocative device
  D High profits will generally attract resources from less remunerative activities

18 The multiplier effect of government investment is likely to be greater where:

  A There is excess prediction capacity in the private sector of industry
  B There is a high marginal propensity to consume
  C The increased spending is financed by higher taxation
  D There is a high level of stock in firms

19 According to the view represented by a Phillips curve, which of the following is correct?

  A Higher inflation causes unemployment
  B Higher unemployment causes inflation
  C Unemployment and inflation are not related
  D Full employment and low inflation cannot be achieved together

20 The total yield from an indirect tax levied on a good is likely to be greatest when:

  A Demand is inelastic, supply is elastic
  B Demand is inelastic, supply is inelastic
  C Demand is elastic, supply is elastic
  D Demand is elastic, supply is inelastic

Mock assessment 1

21 Product T has inelastic demand. The recent introduction of productivity-improving equipment in the manufacture of product T is expected to result, short term, in conditions of excess supply. Which of the following changes will eventually remove the conditions of excess supply?

- A A fall in price that stimulates a large increase in demand
- B A small reduction in price, resulting in a large shift to the left in the supply curve, and so a large fall in demand
- C A large number of firms will leave the industry, and so total supply will fall
- D A large fall in price, creating a fairly small increase in demand and a large fall in supply

22 Which of the following may cause an increase in National Income?

- A A fall in investment
- B A rise in exports
- C An increase in saving
- D A fall in consumer spending

23 A country's economy is experiencing a low rate of economic growth and a high level of technological unemployment. A policy by the government aimed at increasing aggregate demand to raise the rate of growth in National Income would have all of the following effects *except* which *one*?

- A It would be inflationary
- B It would create supply bottlenecks
- C It would worsen the balance of trade
- D It would reduce unemployment

24 Which of the following measures can help to tackle the problem of cost-push inflation?

1. Higher direct taxation
2. Wage increases being linked to productivity improvements
3. Higher interest rates
4. A revaluation of the currency

- A Measures 1, 2 and 3 only
- B Measures 1, 2 and 4 only
- C Measures 2, 3 and 4 only
- D Measures 2 and 4 only

25

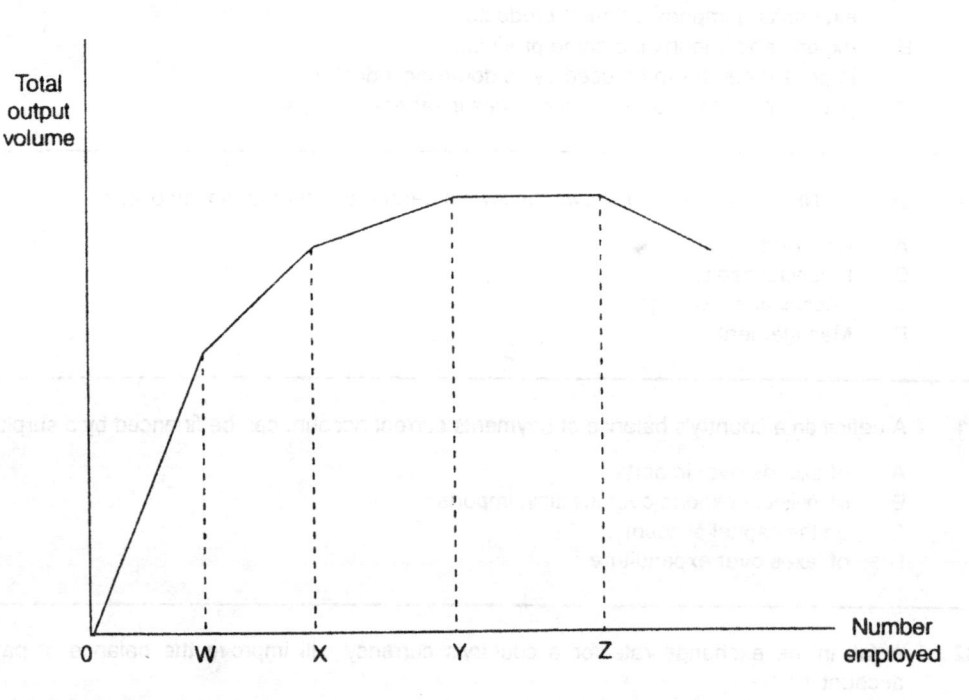

[Diagram: Total output volume against Number employed. Curve rises steeply from 0 to W, rises less steeply from W to X, rises slightly from X to Y, is flat from Y to Z, then falls after Z.]

In the diagram above, from what level of employment do diminishing returns start to occur?

A Above employment level W
B Above employment level X
C Above employment level Y
D Above employment level Z

26 Much Wapping is a small town in Hampshire where a municipal swimming pool and sports centre has just been built by a private firm Hands Bumpsydaisy Ltd. Which of the following is an external benefit of the project?

A The increased trade of local shops
B The increased traffic in the neighbourhood
C The increased profits for the sports firm
D The increased building on previously open land

27 International trade is best explained by the fact that:

A all countries have an absolute advantage in the production of something
B all countries have specialised in the production of certain goods and services
C no country has an absolute advantage in the production of all goods and services
D all countries have a comparative advantage in the production of something

28 All of the following will encourage the process of the globalisation of production except which one?

A Reductions in international transport costs
B Higher levels of tariffs
C Reduced barriers to international capital movements
D Increased similarity in demand patterns between countries

Mock assessment 1

29 Intra-industry trade occurs when a country:

- A exports and imports different products
- B exports and imports the same products
- C imports materials to be used by its domestic industry
- D exports materials for use in industries in other countries

30 Which ONE of the following shows the lowest degree of international mobility?

- A Unskilled labour
- B Financial capital
- C Technical knowledge
- D Management

31 A deficit on a country's balance of payments current account can be financed by a surplus:

- A of exports over imports
- B of invisible exports over invisible imports
- C on the capital account
- D of taxes over expenditure

32 A fall in the exchange rate for a country's currency will improve the balance of payments current account if:

- A the price elasticity of demand for imports is greater than for exports
- B the price elasticity of demand for exports is greater than for imports
- C the sum of the price elasticities for imports and exports is less than one
- D the sum of the price elasticities for imports and exports is greater than one

33 All of the following are benefits which all countries will gain from the adoption of a single currency such as the euro, except which one?

- A Reduced transactions costs
- B Increased price transparency
- C Lower interest rates
- D Reduced exchange rate uncertainty

34 Compared to a fixed exchange rate system, an economy will benefit from a flexible exchange rate system because:

- A it enables businesses to vary their export prices
- B the government will not have to deflate the economy when balance of payments deficits occur
- C it reduces the cost of acquiring foreign exchange
- D it ensures that businesses never become uncompetitive in international markets

35 What determines the opportunity cost of holding money?

- A The rate of growth in the money supply
- B The rate of price inflation
- C The interest rate on deposits
- D The level of economic output

36 Which *one* of the following would be likely to lead to a fall in the value of the UK pound sterling against the euro?

   A   A rise in UK interest rates
   B   A rise in interest rates in the Euro Zone
   C   The UK central bank buying sterling in exchange for euros
   D   Increased capital flows from the Euro Zone to the UK

37 An increase in international mobility of factors of production will cause:

   A   Increasing unemployment in low-wage countries
   B   Increasing differences in wage rates between countries
   C   An increased volume of international trade
   D   Decreasing differences in factor prices between countries

38 Delete the incorrect **bold** word in the sentence below.

   On a production possibility diagram, an increase in productive potential overall is indicated by an **inward/outward** movement of the frontier.

39 Complete the sentence below.

   When demand is elastic, a fall in price will result in a ▓▓▓▓▓▓▓▓▓▓ in total expenditure.

40 The diagram below illustrates the effect of a subsidy on the supplier and consumer of a good. The total amount of the subsidy is the distance AB. Which part of this is received by the consumer of the good?

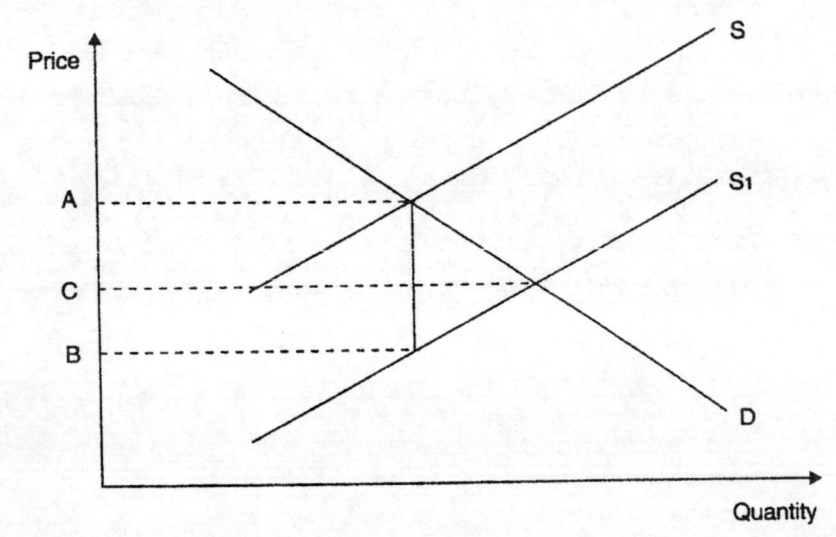

   ☐ AC
   ☐ CB

ANSWERS

**DO NOT TURN THIS PAGE UNTIL YOU
HAVE COMPLETED MOCK ASSESSMENT 1**

Mock assessment 1: answers

1   B   D seems tempting, but it is not as precise as B.

2   D   Tax depends upon tax computations, not economic reality. Don't forget that normal profit is the opportunity cost of enterprise.

3   C   A and D = elastic demand, B = unit elasticity.

4   D   Members of a cartel can locate anywhere.

5   A   This is a point of definition.

6   B   A relates to two different firms and D relates to two different products. C is tempting, but it is the different conditions of supply which lead to the price difference.

7   C   Product differentiation is an important example of non-price competition.

8   D   A and B are not **in themselves** undesirable. C is a political point rather than an economic one.

9   C   Fact.

10   A   The higher the risk, the higher the return.

11   B   Different types of money have differing degrees of liquidity.

12   A   A transfer payment is one not made in return for a productive service.

13   C   Highly mobile capital and labour could themselves move to wherever they were most efficiently employed.

14   D   This would make imports more expensive.

15   A   In the short term, supply is perfectly inelastic and so the same quantity of yachts will be made and sold. Given no change in demand conditions, the price will be unchanged too.

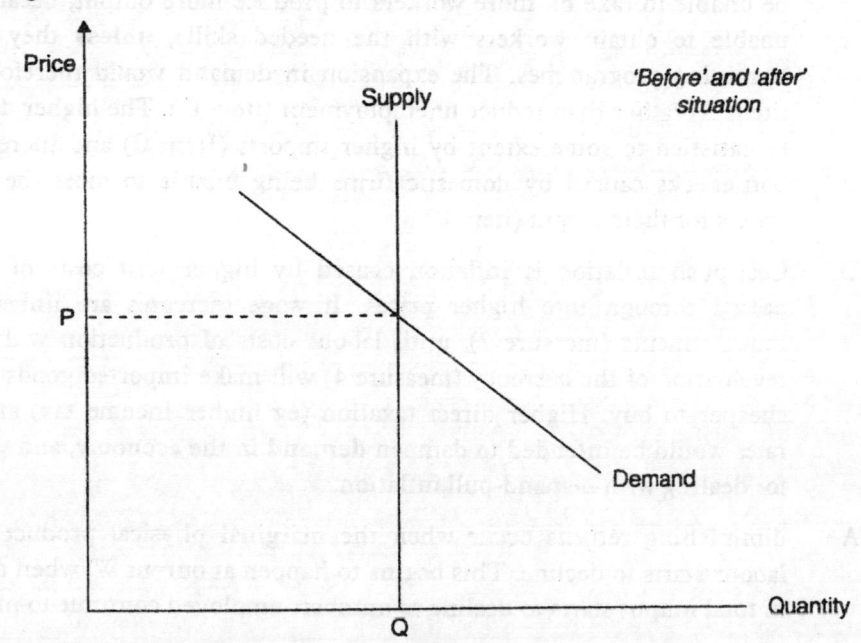

16   B   Economic rent is the surplus of actual earnings for a factor of production over what it could earn in its next best employment (transfer earnings).

17   B   'The consumer is king' only when there are perfect markets and perfect competition. With monopoly, monopolistic competition, oligopoly and imperfect markets, the price mechanism still operated but firms wield some influence and the sovereignty of the consumer is not complete.

Mock assessment 1: answers

18	B	The government investment multiplier will work through to private sector investment (through the government multiplier effect). Excess production capacity in industry (item A) and a high level of stocks (item D), however, will avoid the need for **new** investment by industry. A higher rate of marketing taxation (implied by item C) will reduce the multiplier. A high marketing propensity to consume (item B) helps to keep the multiplier high.
19	D	A Phillips curve shows how lower unemployment can only be achieved in conjunction with higher rates of inflation.
20	B	The total yield from an indirect tax is likely to be greatest when (a) demand for the good is relatively unaffected by the addition of a tax on to the price and (b) supply is relatively unaffected, even though suppliers will be receiving the price net of the tax.
21	D	Demand for goods is inelastic and so large changes in demand will not happen; thus, A and B cannot be correct. Event C **might** occur, but the reasons why this should be so are not explained. Event D seems the most likely outcomes: a large fall in price will be needed to remove excess supply, and this would also cause a small increase in demand.
22	B	Since Y = C + 1 + G + (X – M), a fall in C or I would reduce National Income, but a rise in exports X would increase National Income. Savings are a withdrawal from the circular flow and so would reduce national Income, unless they could be diverted into higher investment.
23	D	Technological unemployment is a form of structural unemployment that occurs when people are put out of work by technological developments, possibly because they do not have the necessary skills to work with the new technology. If the government took measures to increase aggregate demand in the economy, domestic firms would be unable to take on more workers to produce more output, because they would be unable to obtain workers with the needed skills, **unless** they spent money on retraining programmes. The expansion in demand would therefore be inflationary (item A) rather than reduce unemployment (item D). The higher demand would also be satisfied to some extent by higher imports (Item C) and there would be supply bottlenecks caused by domestic firms being unable to meet the larger volume of orders for their output (item B).
24	D	Cost-push inflation is inflation caused by higher unit costs of production being passed through into higher prices. If wage increases are linked to productivity improvements (measure 2), until labour costs of production will be kept down. A revaluation of the currency (measure 4) will make imported goods and raw materials cheaper to buy. Higher direct taxation (eg higher income tax) and higher interest rates would be intended to dampen **demand** in the economy, and would be measures for dealing with demand-pull inflation.
25	A	diminishing returns occur when the marginal physical product of extra units of labour starts to decline. This begins to happen at output W, when the rate of increase in total output starts to decline as numbers employed continue to increase.
26	A	Item B is an external cost of the project, since increased volumes of traffic are harmful to the environment. Item C is a private benefit for the firm. Item D would only be an external benefit if a building is better for society than the use of open land, which is unlikely. Item A is correct because the benefits to local shops are additional to the private benefits of the sports firm and as such are external benefits.
27	D	This is because comparative advantage is measured in opportunity cost terms, not absolute cost terms.

Mock assessment 1: answers

28	B	Clearly, higher tariffs will drive up import prices and thus reduce the volume bought and sold.
29	B	This is a definition.
30	A	Financial capital can be transferred electronically, as, to some extent, can technical knowledge. Technological workers and managers both have skills that are internationally applicable and the money to pay for travel.
31	C	The balance of payments current account deals with imports and exports, so A and B are nonsensical and D is irrelevant.
32	D	The improvement is dependent on a rise in exports and a fall in imports in response to price changes. Demand for both must be reasonably elastic if this is to occur.
33	C	A single interest rate is set for the whole euro bloc. Inevitably, some joiners will have existing rates that are greater than this, and some will have lower rates.
34	B	Export prices will only change if the rate changes. Exchange dealing costs remain the same. There is far more to international competitiveness than the exchange rate. Also, a floating exchange rate is affected by factors other than trade performance; these include the interest rate in particular.
35	C	The interest rate is the opportunity cost.
36	B	This will make sterling less attractive to hold.
37	D	With lower barriers, factor price differences will lessen.
38	'Inward' is incorrect.	
39	Rise.	
40	AC. The equilibrium price falls from A to C.	

Foundation

MOCK ASSESSMENT 2

Paper 3a

Economics for Business

FECB

You are allowed one hour to answer this assessment.

Answer ALL questions

DO NOT OPEN THIS PAPER UNTIL YOU ARE READY
TO START UNDER EXAMINATION CONDITIONS

Mock assessment 2

1 The 'central economic problem' is:

   A   the persistence of unemployment.
   B   the need to allocate scarce resources between competing uses.
   C   consumers having less money than they would like.
   D   the need to ensure that in the long run all production costs are covered by sales revenue

2 Which *one* of the following would shift a country's production possibility frontier (PPF) *outwards* (away from the origin)?

   A   A fall in unemployment
   B   An increase in exports
   C   A rise in total consumer expenditure
   D   Technical progress reducing production costs

3 The term 'rising economic welfare' means:

   A   an increase in state welfare payments.
   B   a rising standard of living.
   C   increased employment opportunities
   D   increased consumption of health and education services

4 If an economy experiences an 'increase in productivity', this means that:

   A   the level of total output in the economy has risen
   B   employees are working harder than before
   C   output per unit of input has risen
   D   technical change has taken place

5 Which *one* of the following is *not* an example of an external social cost?

   A   Reduction of oil reserves owing to increased use of cars
   B   River pollution caused by a manufacturing process
   C   Health problems caused by vehicle emissions
   D   Discarded packaging outside fast-food outlets

6 All of the following government policies would tend to raise the long-term rate of economic growth *except* which *one*?

   A   Encouraging a higher level of business investment
   B   Increasing expenditure on education and training
   C   Encouraging a higher level of consumer expenditure
   D   Providing tax relief for research and development expenditure by businesses

7 Which *one* of the following is a feature of a market economy?

   A   Prices are determined mainly by market forces
   B   Resources are allocated between different markets by administrative decisions
   C   Consumer preferences are determined by market research
   D   All markets are characterised by a high degree of competition.

8 The demand curve for the product of a business will shift to the right when there is:

   A   a reduction in indirect tax on the good
   B   an improvement in production which lowers costs
   C   a fall in the price of the good
   D   an increase in the supply of a complementary good

131

Mock assessment 2

9 If the demand for a firm's product has a price elasticity of –2, a 10 per cent *fall* in its price will:

    A   decrease total revenue by 20 per cent
    B   increase sales volume by 10 per cent
    C   increase sales volume by 20 per cent
    D   increase total revenue by 20 per cent

10 The short-run average-cost curve for firms rises after a certain level of output because of:

    A   diseconomies of scale
    B   the law of diminishing returns
    C   diminishing marginal utility
    D   rising price of factors of production

11 The imposition of a minimum wage will cause unemployment in a labour market only if:

    A   the demand for labour is elastic
    B   the demand for labour is inelastic
    C   the minimum wage is above the equilibrium wage
    D   the minimum wage is below the equilibrium wage

12 Government may be concerned about the growth of monopoly power in an industry because monopolies:

    A   attempt to maximise profits
    B   restrict output
    C   may secure economies of scale
    D   control a large share of the market

13 Which *one* of the following will tend to *increase* the degree of competition in an industry?

    A   Product differentiation
    B   Horizontal integration
    C   Economies of scale
    D   Low fixed costs

14 Which *one* of the following is *not* a factor of production?

    A   Unskilled labour
    B   A machine tool
    C   Cash reserves
    D   Entrepreneurship

15 In oligopolistic industries, *interdependence of decision-making* arises because:

    A   the effect of decisions by one firm depends on the reactions of others
    B   there is heavy advertising of products
    C   firms always find it more profitable to collude than to compete
    D   the reaction of rival firms is uncertain

16 In calculating national income, double-counting can be avoided by:

    A   deducting taxes and adding subsidies
    B   deducting imports and adding exports
    C   excluding the value of the output of intermediate goods
    D   excluding the value of transactions in second hand goods.

17 A rise in interest rate in a country can be expected to lead to all of the following except which one?

- A A fall in share prices
- B A rise in investment
- C A rise in the exchange rate
- D A shift of income from borrowers to savers

18 Which one of the following is not a normal feature of the upswing phase of the trade cycle?

- A Falling unemployment
- B Rising levels of imports
- C Rising national income
- D Increasing government borrowing

19 Governments wish to control inflation because it:

- A tends to reduce government tax revenue
- B causes the money supply to expand
- C damages international competitiveness
- D shifts income towards holders of financial assets

20 Structural unemployment is caused by:

- A long-term decline in demand for an industry's products
- B falling levels of aggregate demand
- C high levels of inflation
- D a downturn in national economic activity

21 Which one of the following would be part of a supply-side policy to reduce unemployment in an economy?

- A Reducing the supply of imports by raising trade barriers
- B Increasing labour retraining schemes
- C Public expenditure to increase the supply of merit goods
- D Supplying government subsidies to declining industries

22 Which one of the following will appear in the capital account (transactions in assets and liabilities) of the balance of payments?

- A Export of a manufactured good
- B Expenditure by a citizen on foreign holiday
- C Interest received on an overseas investment
- D Inflow of investment into the country from an overseas company

23 Which one of the following is not a benefit of adopting a single currency within a trading bloc of countries?

- A A reduction in international transactions costs
- B The elimination of exchange rate uncertainty
- C The ability for each country to adopt an independent monetary policy
- D Increased international price transparency

Mock assessment 2

24 If the exchange rate for a country's currency fell, the result would be that export prices:

- A measured in the domestic currency would fall
- B measured in the domestic currency would rise
- C measured in foreign currency would fall
- D measured in foreign currency would rise

25 Which one of the following is not associated with the process of the globalisation of production?

- A Rising trade ratios for economies
- B Concentration of production close to markets
- C Increasing production by transnational corporations
- D Increased international factor mobility

26 The 'free rider' problem occurs when:

- A an attempt is made to tax negative externalities
- B an attempt is made to charge for a public good
- C an attempt is made to charge for a merit good
- D an indirect tax is applied selectively

27 In economics, the term opportunity cost refers to:

- A the monetary cost of a good or service
- B the cost of producing the goods measured in money terms
- C the monetary cost of acquiring a factor of production
- D the value of a good or service foregone

28 The importance of saving in promoting economic growth is because of its relationship with:

- A present consumption
- B future consumption
- C investment
- D interest rates

29 Economic growth is desirable because it makes all of the following possible EXCEPT which ONE?

- A The elimination of the economic problem
- B Higher living standards
- C Increased private and public consumption
- D Increased leisure

30 All of the following policies would promote export-led economic growth EXCEPT which ONE?

- A A reduction in the country's tariffs on imports
- B A restrictive domestic monetary policy
- C The removal of taxes on employing labour
- D An appreciation in the country's foreign exchange rate

31 Economic growth in developed economies tends to be associated with

- A a reduction in the output of the industrial sector in the economy
- B a rise in the importance of the service sector in the economy
- C a reduction in the dependence on imports
- D a rise in the number of workers in the primary sector

134

Mock assessment 2

32 Economies of scale are best described as the process by which

- A large, dominant firms can secure higher profits
- B large firms can better organise their factors of production
- C large-scale production permits the use of new technology
- D large-scale production leads to lower costs per unit of output

33 Which ONE of the following will tend to make the demand for a company's product LESS price elastic?

- A A rise in consumer incomes
- B A rise in the price of complementary goods
- C A fall in the number of substitute goods
- D A lower price for the good

34 Which ONE of the following does NOT restrict the number of firms in an industry?

- A Low levels of product differentiation
- B Significant economies of scale
- C Barriers to entry
- D The use of capital-intensive technology in the industry

35 An airline sells standby passenger tickets at a much lower price than tickets bought in advance. This is because:

- A marginal cost is low for a seat up to the point where an aeroplane is fully occupied
- B the average cost of a standby seat is lower than its marginal cost
- C selling additional tickets in this way will raise average revenue
- D the demand for seats is always price-inelastic

36 The real rate of interest:

- A Is the rate charged on loans
- B Is the yield on irredeemable government stocks
- C Equals the nominal interest rate minus the rate of inflation
- D Is the rate most relevant in making lending decisions

37 Which ONE of the following is an example of a non-tariff barrier?

- A Price differences caused by import duties
- B Differences in regulations between countries which prevent free trade
- C Import duties
- D Reductions in domestic production resulting from increased imports from low-cost countries

38 Complete the sentence below.

A fall in demand for a good is likely to cause a ▓▓▓▓▓▓▓▓▓▓ in demand for another good that is a complement.

39 A straight line demand curve displays constant elasticity at all points along its length.

☐ True

☐ False

Mock assessment 2

40 A supply curve will shift to the right if there is a rise in the price of other goods.

☐ True

☐ False

ANSWERS

DO NOT TURN THIS PAGE UNTIL YOU
HAVE COMPLETED MOCK ASSESSMENT 2

Mock assessment 2: answers

1 A The allocation of scarce resources is the essence of economics.

2 D A fall in unemployment would move output towards the PPC from within. An increase in exports is merely a change in the pattern of consumption. A rise in consumer spending would lead to inflation if output was already on the PPC.

3 B Economic welfare is about consumption of all kinds (except demerit goods).

4 C A could happen without a productivity increase; for example, more resources might become available. B would be one way productivity could rise, but is not the only way. Productivity increases can follow from technical improvements, but this is not the only source.

5 A Depletion of oil reserves is a consequence internal to the sale of oil; the other items are external to the economic transactions that bring them about, that is, they affect people who are not parties to the transactions.

6 C A, B and D will affect supply and move the PPC outwards. C is a demand measure and can only help if the economy is under-performing. If the economy is producing at its maximum potential, increasing demand alone will lead to inflation rather than growth.

7 A B is typical of a planned economy. D is not a state of affairs that can realistically be expected – the existence of natural monopolies alone would ensure that. C describes an attempt to anticipate market forces.

8 D A and B will affect supply, C will change the quantity demanded by a move along the demand curve.

9 C A and D are incorrect because elasticity is by definition about **quantity demanded**. B is arithmetically incorrect.

10 B A is a long run effect. C determines the shape of the demand curve. D is wrong because the theory of short run costs assumes stable prices.

11 C D is simply wrong. B is plausible, but the demand curve would have to be vertical, that is **perfectly** inelastic, which is not a real world condition at all.

12 B A, C and D can be true of many firms that do not approach monopoly power. B is true but to some extent incomplete: monopolies restrict output to maximise their profit and this has undesirable consequences such as higher prices than under perfect competition and lower allocative efficiency.

13 D A and C form barriers to entry. B reduces the number of firms trading in the market. D makes entry into the market and exit from it easy.

14 C Money can be used to acquire factors of production but is not itself a factor.

15 A B is a separate characteristic typical of oligopolies. C is not always true where collusion is illegal; even where firms do not collude they must consider their competitors' reactions to any change in their own pricing policy. D is not entirely true: reactions to price changes are largely predictable, though not in detail.

Mock assessment 2: answers

16	C	B adjusts total domestic expenditure to GDP at market prices and A converts GDP at market price to GDP at factor cost, when using the expenditure approach. Trading in second hand goods is a value-adding service.
17	B	Higher interest rates make borrowing to invest more expensive.
18	D	Tax revenues increase and welfare payments decrease during the upswing, so a higher proportion of government spending can be funded from tax.
19	C	Inflation will cause money value revenue to rise; revenue in real terms will not change. Expansion of the money supply may lead to inflation rather than vice versa. Inflation reduces the real value of both financial assets and the income they produce.
20	A	B is demand deficient unemployment, as is D. Inflation is usually associated with excess demand and therefore with rising employment.
21	B	A would not really affect supply or demand. C is actually an increase in demand for a particular type of good. D would tend to prevent improvements in supply by protecting the *status quo*.
22	D	Capital account is concerned with investment flows. A, B and C are all current account items.
23	C	This is impossible with a single currency.
24	C	They would remain the same in domestic currency.
25	B	This is actually debatable.
26	B	Fact.
27	D	This is a definition.
28	C	Present consumption is reduced by saving: this reduction in demand can have a negative effect on growth as in Japan 1990-2002. Saving can provide for future consumption but the extent to which consumption increases in the future will promote growth is debateable. High levels of saving *may* exert some downward pressure on interest rates or, at least, modify an upward pressure, but this effect is likely to be very small.
29	A	People's wants will never be satisfied.
30	D	This would make exports more expensive to buy. A might encourage reciprocal treatment by other countries. B would reduce domestic demand, making more goods available for export. C would reduce the cost and hence, possibly, the price of exports.
31	B	The manufacturing sector's output may well remain constant, as may that of the primary sector. Indeed, employment in agricultural in particular may decline as labour saving devices replace expensive people. C is debateable: there is likely to be growth in both imports and exports.
32	D	This is a definition, almost.

Mock assessment 2: answers

33 A D will simply demonstrate the elasticity that is present. B and C may shift the demand curve but are unlikely to affect its elasticity.

34 A Scale economies and the need for heavy investment are themselves barriers to entry, since they demand major capital resources to overcome. The lower the degree of differentiation, the closer the approach is to perfect competition.

35 A The plane will fly anyway: carrying an extra passenger costs little.

36 C The real rate of interest is the amount by which nominal rates exceed inflation.

37 B Sometimes, excessive 'red tape' regulations might be deliberately imposed as a means of protection.

38 Fall. Complements are goods that are consumed together.

39 False.

40 False. The production of the good will be less attractive if the price of other goods rises. Less will be offered at any price.

See overleaf for information on other
BPP products and how to order

CIMA Order

To BPP Professional Education, Aldine Place, London W12 8AW
Tel: 020 8740 2211 Fax: 020 8740 1184
email: publishing@bpp.com
Order online: www.bpp.com

Mr/Mrs/Ms (Full name) _____

Daytime delivery address _____

Postcode _____

Daytime Tel _____ Email _____

Date of exam (month/year) _____

Occasionally we may wish to email you relevant offers and information about courses and products.
Please tick to opt into this service. ☐

POSTAGE & PACKING

Study Texts

	First	Each extra	Online
UK	£5.00	£2.00	£
Europe*	£6.00	£4.00	£
Rest of world	£20.00	£10.00	£

Kits

	First	Each extra	Online
UK	£5.00	£2.00	£
Europe*	£6.00	£4.00	£
Rest of world	£20.00	£10.00	£

Passcards/Success Tapes/MCQ Cards/CDs

	First	Each extra	Online
UK	£2.00	£1.00	£
Europe*	£3.00	£2.00	£
Rest of world	£8.00	£8.00	£

Grand Total (incl. Postage) £ _____

I enclose a cheque for ☐☐☐☐☐☐☐☐
(Cheques to BPP Professional Education)

Or charge to Visa/Mastercard/Switch

Card Number ☐☐☐☐☐☐☐☐☐☐☐☐☐☐☐☐

Expiry date ☐☐☐☐   Start Date ☐☐☐☐

Issue Number (Switch Only) ☐

Signature _____

Order Items

		7/03 Texts	1/04 Kits	1/04 Passcards	Success Tapes	Success CDs	Virtual Campus	7/03 I-Pass	7/03 I-Learn	5/03 MCQ cards
FOUNDATION										
1	Financial Accounting Fundamentals	£20.95 ☐	£10.95 ☐	£6.95 ☐	£12.95 ☐	£14.95 ☐	£50 ☐	£24.95 ☐		£5.95 ☐
2	Management Accounting Fundamentals	£20.95 ☐	£10.95 ☐	£6.95 ☐	£12.95 ☐	£14.95 ☐	£50 ☐	£24.95 ☐		£5.95 ☐
3A	Economics for Business	£20.95 ☐	£10.95 ☐	£6.95 ☐	£12.95 ☐	£14.95 ☐	£50 ☐	£24.95 ☐		£5.95 ☐
3B	Business Law	£20.95 ☐	£10.95 ☐	£6.95 ☐	£12.95 ☐	£14.95 ☐	£50 ☐	£24.95 ☐		£5.95 ☐
3C	Business Mathematics	£20.95 ☐	£10.95 ☐	£6.95 ☐	£12.95 ☐	£14.95 ☐	£50 ☐	£24.95 ☐		£5.95 ☐
INTERMEDIATE									7/03	
4	Finance	£20.95 ☐	£10.95 ☐	£6.95 ☐	£12.95 ☐	£14.95 ☐	£90 ☐	£24.95 ☐	£34.95 ☐	£5.95 ☐
5	Business Tax (FA 2003) (10/03)	£20.95 ☐	£10.95 ☐	£6.95 ☐	£12.95 ☐	£14.95 ☐	£90 ☐	£24.95 ☐	£34.95 ☐	£5.95 ☐
6	Financial Accounting	£20.95 ☐	£10.95 ☐	£6.95 ☐	£12.95 ☐	£14.95 ☐	£90 ☐	£24.95 ☐	£34.95 ☐	£5.95 ☐
6i	Financial Accounting International	£20.95 ☐	£10.95 ☐	£6.95 ☐	£12.95 ☐	£14.95 ☐	£90 ☐	£24.95 ☐		£5.95 ☐
7	Financial Reporting	£20.95 ☐	£10.95 ☐	£6.95 ☐	£12.95 ☐	£14.95 ☐	£90 ☐	£24.95 ☐	£34.95 ☐	£5.95 ☐
7i	Financial Reporting International	£20.95 ☐	£10.95 ☐	£6.95 ☐	£12.95 ☐	£14.95 ☐	£90 ☐	£24.95 ☐		£5.95 ☐
8	Management Accounting - Performance Management	£20.95 ☐	£10.95 ☐	£6.95 ☐	£12.95 ☐	£14.95 ☐	£90 ☐	£24.95 ☐	£34.95 ☐	£5.95 ☐
9	Management Accounting - Decision Making	£20.95 ☐	£10.95 ☐	£6.95 ☐	£12.95 ☐	£14.95 ☐	£90 ☐	£24.95 ☐	£34.95 ☐	£5.95 ☐
10	Systems and Project Management	£20.95 ☐	£10.95 ☐	£6.95 ☐	£12.95 ☐	£14.95 ☐	£90 ☐	£24.95 ☐	£34.95 ☐	£5.95 ☐
11	Organisational Management	£20.95 ☐	£10.95 ☐	£6.95 ☐	£12.95 ☐	£14.95 ☐	£90 ☐	£24.95 ☐	£34.95 ☐	£5.95 ☐
FINAL										
12	Management Accounting - Business Strategy	£20.95 ☐	£10.95 ☐	£6.95 ☐	£12.95 ☐	£14.95 ☐		£24.95 ☐		
13	Management Accounting - Financial Strategy	£20.95 ☐	£10.95 ☐	£6.95 ☐	£12.95 ☐	£14.95 ☐		£24.95 ☐		
14	Management Accounting - Information Strategy	£20.95 ☐	£10.95 ☐	£6.95 ☐	£12.95 ☐	£14.95 ☐		£24.95 ☐		
15	Case Study (1) Workbook (2) Toolkit	£20.95 ☐	£20.95 ☐ (For 5/04: available 3/04. For 11/04: available 9/04)		£12.95 ☐	£14.95 ☐				
	Learning to Learn Accountancy (7/02)	£9.95 ☐								

Total _____

We aim to deliver to all UK addresses inside 5 working days. A signature will be required. Orders to all EU addresses should be delivered within 8 working days. *Europe includes the Republic of Ireland and the Channel Islands.

CIMA – Foundation Paper 3a Economics for Business (1/04)

REVIEW FORM & FREE PRIZE DRAW

All original review forms from the entire BPP range, completed with genuine comments, will be entered into one of two draws on 31 July 2004 and 31 January 2005. The names on the first four forms picked out on each occasion will be sent a cheque for £50.

Name: _____   Address: _____

How have you used this Kit?
(Tick one box only)

- [ ] Self study (book only)
- [ ] On a course: college (please state) _____
- [ ] With 'correspondence' package
- [ ] Other _____

Why did you decide to purchase this Kit?
(Tick one box only)

- [ ] Have used the complementary Study Text
- [ ] Have used other BPP products in the past
- [ ] Recommendation by friend/colleague
- [ ] Recommendation by a lecturer at college
- [ ] Saw advertising
- [ ] Saw website
- [ ] Other _____

During the past six months do you recall seeing/receiving any of the following?
(Tick as many boxes as are relevant)

- [ ] Our advertisement in *CIMA Insider*
- [ ] Our advertisement in *Financial Management*
- [ ] Our advertisement in *Pass*
- [ ] Our advertisement in *PQ*
- [ ] Our brochure with a letter through the post
- [ ] Our website

Which (if any) aspects of our advertising do you find useful?
(Tick as many boxes as are relevant)

- [ ] Prices and publication dates of new editions
- [ ] Information on product content
- [ ] Facility to order books off-the-page
- [ ] None of the above

When did you sit the exam? _____

Which of the following BPP products have you used for this paper?

- [ ] Study Text
- [ ] MCQ Cards
- [x] Kit
- [ ] Passcards
- [ ] Success Tape
- [ ] Success CD
- [ ] i-Products

Your ratings, comments and suggestions would be appreciated on the following areas of this Kit.

	Very useful	Useful	Not useful
Effective revision and revision plan	☐	☐	☐
Exam guidance	☐	☐	☐
Background (Websites and mindmap)	☐	☐	☐
Preparation questions	☐	☐	☐
Exam standard questions	☐	☐	☐
'Pass marks' section in answers	☐	☐	☐
Content and structure of answers	☐	☐	☐
Mock exams	☐	☐	☐
'Plan of attack'	☐	☐	☐
Mock exam answers	☐	☐	☐

	Excellent	Good	Adequate	Poor
Overall opinion of this Kit	☐	☐	☐	☐

Do you intend to continue using BPP products?   ☐ Yes   ☐ No

Please note any further comments and suggestions/errors on the reverse of this page. The BPP author of this edition can be e-mailed at: rogerpeskett@bpp.com

Please return this form to: Nick Weller, CIMA range manager, BPP Professional Education, FREEPOST, London, W12 8BR

CIMA – Foundation Paper 3a Economics for Business (1/04)

REVIEW FORM & FREE PRIZE DRAW (continued)

Please note any further comments and suggestions/errors below.

FREE PRIZE DRAW RULES

1. Closing date for 31 July 2004 draw is 30 June 2004. Closing date for 31 January 2005 draw is 31 December 2004.

2. Restricted to entries with UK and Eire addresses only. BPP employees, their families and business associates are excluded.

3. No purchase necessary. Entry forms are available upon request from BPP Professional Education. No more than one entry per title, per person. Draw restricted to persons aged 16 and over.

4. Winners will be notified by post and receive their cheques not later than 6 weeks after the relevant draw date.

5. The decision of the promoter in all matters is final and binding. No correspondence will be entered into.